Training Sessions For Soccer Coaches - Volume 1

Coaching Soccer, Volume 1

Chris King

Published by Chris King, 2023.

TRAINING SESSIONS FOR SOCCER COACHES - VOLUME 1

First edition. April 25, 2023.

ISBN: 979-8223827320

Written by Chris King.

TRAINING SESSIONS FOR

SOCCER COACHES

VOLUME 1

Coaching Books For Amateur Soccer Coaches

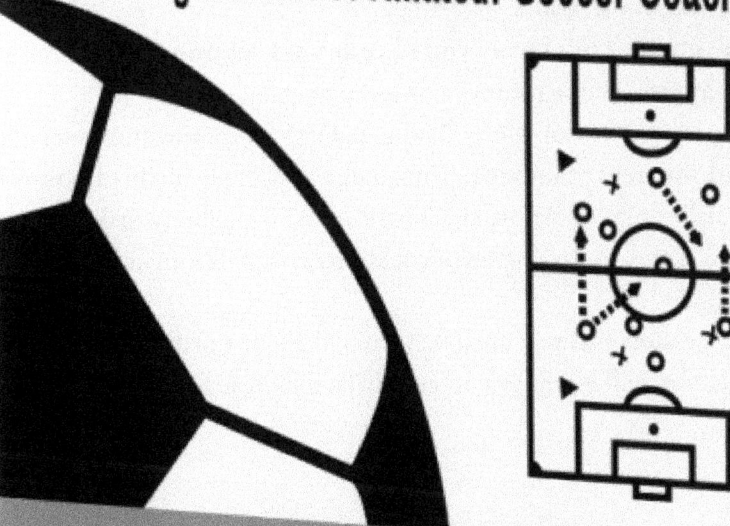

CHRIS KING

TRAINING SESSIONS FOR SOCCER COACHES - VOLUME 1

CHAPTER 1

INTRODUCTION

This book is for non-professional soccer coaches who want to improve their training sessions (and in turn their match day performance from their team).

"Training Sessions for Soccer Coaches - Book 1" lays out full training sessions that will improve different parts of your team's game. **It walks you through what to do from the warm up to the warm down and all the drills in between.**

The drills in this book are explained step by step and include diagrams. They will have you running a quality training session in no time. The drills are aimed at senior players (but they can be adjusted for juniors aged approximately 13 years and up).

These training sessions have been chosen because they work in real life, not just in a book. I have played and coached for over 30 years and I ran these sessions last season. These drills will bring improvement and better results to you and your team.

These drills are 100% on the ball so they improve endurance, technique, and tactics all at the same time plus you'll see your players enjoying the sessions more.

If you're a new coach, or you're simply a coach that hasn't had the time to work on your sessions, this book will improve you immensely. Game day results start on the training track and if the coach doesn't have a good training session planned, the players won't improve and will lose motivation.

Most drills can be adjusted to suit the number of players you have at your session. I understand that on any night player numbers vary, so most of these drills are adjustable for more or less players.

I've completed coaching courses and coached senior men's teams, ladies, youth and junior teams so I have a well rounded knowledge of different teams and different standards. The advice and drills in this book will get you up and running straight away. Don't jump on YouTube an hour before training looking for a fancy drill - simply choose a session from this book, follow the step by step guides and you will see your sessions and coaching ability improve straight away (plus you'll enjoy coaching more!).

The drills focus on one main aspect per session and you are given three different drills per session that build on each other. In this, my first soccer coaching book, you will learn how to run drills for these four key components of the game:

1. **Supporting The Attack**
2. **Pressing**
3. **Midfield Play**
4. **Playing Out From The Back**

Also in this book you'll also find general advice on things that help your session run smoother which will give you confidence as a coach. Some of it might not seem important, but over a season they will save you time and you will become more organised.

The drills are all aimed at improving players technical ability and all of the drills are 'on the ball'. I believe in getting fit and improving skill through football based drills, not just running for the sake of running. As a coach, you may only have the players for two 90 minute sessions a week, so the training sessions laid out in this book help you get maximum value out of those sessions.

Before you jump into the first session, please spend 5 minutes reading the following chapter which breaks down how a general training session should be structured.

And if you need other coaching books have a look below. I have full coaching sessions for senior players down to coaching kids soccer for parents or volunteers. Just search for:

"Chris King Soccer Coach" or follow the links below:

Or sign up for a free soccer eBook at www.chriskingsoccercoach.com[1]

1. http://www.chriskingsoccercoach.com

VIEW OTHER SOCCER COACHING BOOKS BY CHRIS KING

Training Sessions For Soccer Coaches Volume 1
Training Sessions For Soccer Coaches Volume 2
Training Sessions For Soccer Coaches Volume 3
Attacking & Shooting Drills For Soccer Coaches
Soccer Rondos Volume 1
Soccer Rondos Volume 2
Coaching Kids Soccer - Volume 1
Coaching Kids Soccer - Volume 2
Coaching Kids Soccer - Volume 3

CHAPTER 2
TRAINING SESSION STRUCTURE

A training session with a non-professional senior team should run for approximately 90 minutes (not including initial warm up or warm down). Let's break it down into an average Tuesday night training session at my club.

I realise some coaches may only have an hour or so with their teams so in this case you may want to knock 5 minutes off each of numbers 1,4,5,6 and 7 and if possible, encourage them to get there earlier and do their own light warm up.

Listed below is how I run my session so you can get an idea...

1. 6:00 - 6:10: Players Ready To Go (Light Warm Up)

2. 6:10 - 6:15: Training Starts: Coach Short Introduction Talk

3. 6:15 - 6:35: Warm up (the FIFA 11+[1])

4. 6:35 - 6:55: Drill 1 (Rondo)

5. 7:00 - 7:20: Drill 2 (Positioning Game)

6. 7:20 - 7:40: Drill 3 (Game Training)

7. 7:40 - 8:05: Game (Match Practice)

8. 8:05 - 8:10: Warm Down

Numbers 4,5 and 6 (Drills 1,2 and 3) are the drills that change from session to session and are all covered in detail in this book.

1. PLAYERS READY TO GO (Light Warm Up):

The players should be changed, ready and doing individual light warm ups (foam roller, band stretching, etc) while talking to each other about how well they played on the weekend.

2. TRAINING STARTS: COACHES SHORT INTRODUCTION TALK:

A short 5 minute talk by the coach (you!) on the areas that will be covered in tonight's session (this helps you get player 'buy in' for the session. Players start to understand they're here to learn and work hard, alongside having fun).

3. WARM UP:

The Warm Up should be the FIFA[2] 11+[3] every time (and most parts of this should be performed before a match as well). It has been proven to reduce injuries and players chat and bond at the same time.

4. DRILL 1 (RONDO):

Next is always Drill 1 which is referred to as a Rondo (a simple short, sharp drill that gets the players body and mind warmed up for the session). This runs for approximately 15-20 minutes.

5. DRILL 2 (POSITIONING GAME):

Drill 2 is referred to as a Positioning Game. It is used to get the players thinking about where they should be on the pitch. The drill is in a small area so they get lots of chances to repeat the parts that are being worked on. This should run for approximately 20 minutes.

6. DRILL 3 (GAME TRAINING):

Drill 3 is referred to as Game Training. It is usually an expanded version of Drill 2 in a larger and more match realistic situation. This should run for appropriately 20 minutes.

7. GAME:

It does what it says on the tin - it's time for a game (11v11, 5v5, whatever your numbers are). At the end of the night you should always have a Game. It's great to do drills but eventually it's got to be implemented in a match situation, so this is when you do it. There shouldn't be many (if any) restrictions. Let your players play and hopefully they implement what you have been working on in the session. Look for key moments from the session that night that you have been working on that appear during the game.

---

1. **https://www.youtube.com/watch?v=RSJIp7e7fyY**
2. https://www.youtube.com/watch?v=RSJIp7e7fyY
3. https://www.youtube.com/watch?v=RSJIp7e7fyY

Then stop the game briefly to point out what they are doing correctly or incorrectly. But generally just let the game flow and observe your players.

8. WARM DOWN:

The warm down should be 10 minutes of light jogging, walking and intermittent static stretching.

So that's a general overview of what a training session should look like.

That's enough for now, I'm sure you want to start looking through the first drills, so read on and use my session plans and watch your coaching improve!

Please Note: There's an index at the back of the book for a few terms that will pop up that you may not be familiar with. Plus the FIFA 11+ Warm Up is covered towards the end of the book.

CHAPTER 3

SESSION 1 - SUPPORTING THE ATTACK

Parts of the players game that will be improved from this session:

Supporting the attack; Pressing; Conditioning (fitness); Midfield players movement and awareness; Shooting.

SESSION 1 DRILL 1:
RONDO - PASSING & SHORT COMBINATION PLAY

PURPOSE:

- Improving passing in tight areas and improving the press.

SET UP:

- 10 Players (alternatively 6,8 or 12 players)
- 6 Cones
- 15 x 30 yards
- 15 Minutes

THE DRILL:

- Two teams of 5 players in each half.

- The ball begins with the Black team who attempt to pass and maintain possession.

- Once the first pass is made, one player from the White team (White #1 in this example) can press (creating a 5v1) and attempt to win the ball.

- Every 3 passes equal a goal and after each goal another player from the White team may enter to support the press (ie 5v2 once 3 passes [a goal] are made, 5v3 once 6 passes [2 goals] are made).

- If the White defenders win possession (or the ball goes out of play), they pass back into their waiting teammates in the opposite half and start passing and Black send a player in to create a 5v1.

KEY POINTS:

- Quality of the pass and make sure the attackers spread out.
- Split the defenders with the pass if possible.
- 1 or 2 touch maximum.

COACHES NOTES:

- Play can continue for 2 minutes and the team with the most goals wins, or alternatively the first team to 5 goals wins.

- Have spare balls spread around the outside for continuous, quick play.

- Tell defenders not to get split by a pass as this would take two players out of the action in a real game situation.

- Tell attackers to move the ball quickly, spread out, keep their heads up and split defenders where possible.

CHANGES/PROGRESSION:

- This drill works well with 3v3 and up to 6v6. Change the width of the field accordingly.

Starting Shape: 5v5. Black start in possession and as soon as Black #1 makes the first pass, a White (in this case White #1) runs into the other half to try and win possession. Once Black makes 3 passes another White can enter to help their team mate win possession and so on. (Image: Session 1 - drill 1)

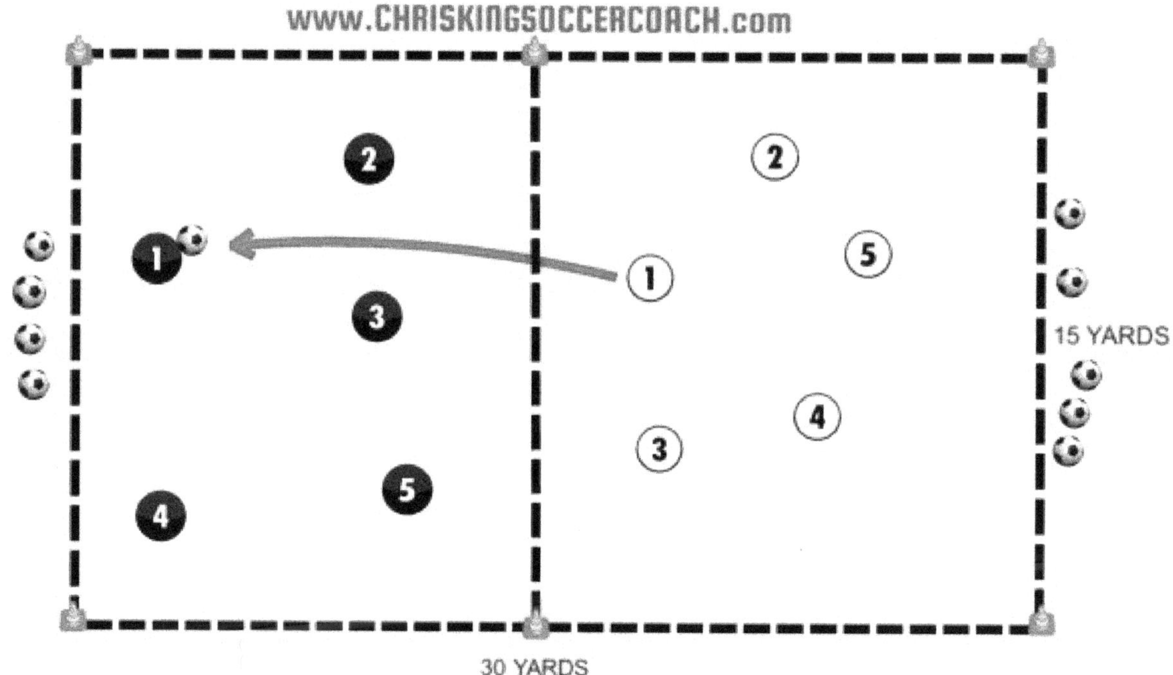

In Play: Blacks have made 3 passes so now another White team mate (White #3) can go across and help with the press.

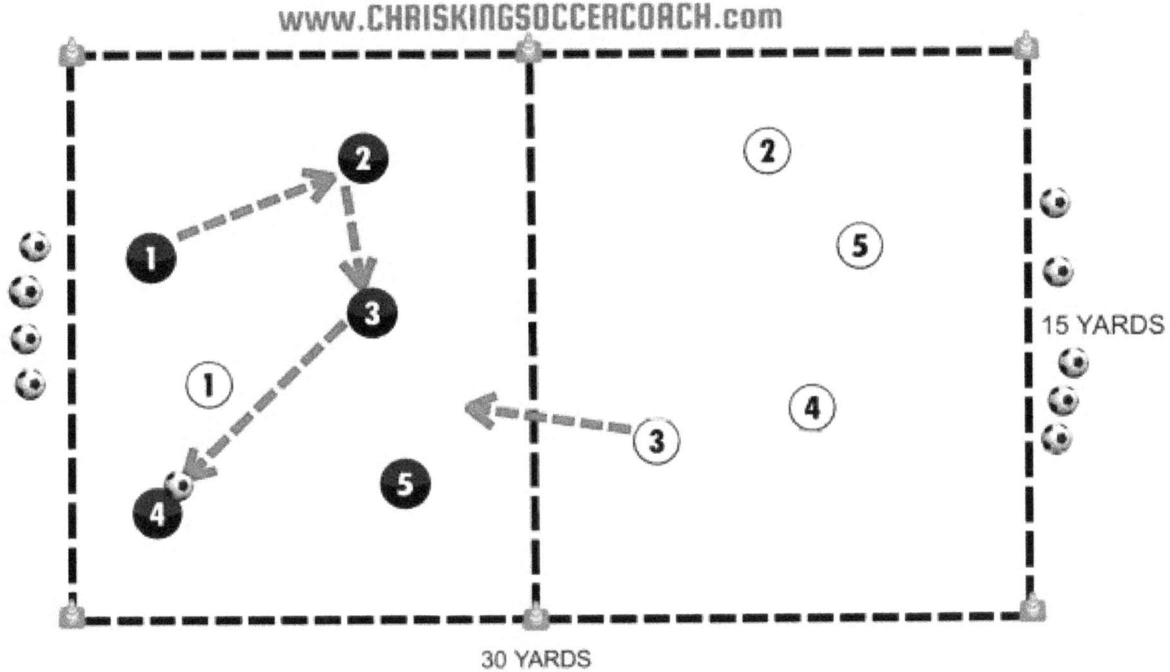

CHAPTER 4
SESSION 1 DRILL 2:
OVERLOADING AREAS TO PLAY FORWARD

PURPOSE:

- Overload the midfield and support the forward player when the ball goes forward.

SET UP:

- 11 Players (alternatively 9 or 13 players - add 2 more in zone B, or for 9 players remove the two outside players)
- 4 Cones + 4 discs
- 15x30 yard area
- 20 minutes

THE DRILL:

- In Zones A & C, it is 1v1 with both Blacks and White locked in their zones.
- In Zone B, it is 2v2+3 (when in possession it becomes 5v2 with the two outside #5 players and middle player #6.
- The 2 #5 outside players may move along the line in Zone B and are on the side of the team in possession.
- When in possession, one of the midfielders in Zone B (Blacks in this case) must move into the other zones (Zones A & C) creating a 2v1 situation. This makes the players support the striker and move forward with the pass.
- The purpose of the game is to move the ball from one target player at one end to the other at the other end, keeping good possession of the ball. For example, once Black #1 in Zone A has gained possession and a player from his team has entered Zone A to support (even if that player doesn't get used), the Blacks try and move it to through Zone B to Black #4 in Zone C.
- If the defenders (White) win the ball, they try to move it from end to end the same as the Blacks.

KEY POINTS:

- Patience in possession.
- Use depth, width and length.

- Expose the overload by using the spare players.

COACHES NOTES:

- Continuous play, swap overload players (#5's & #6) every few minutes.
- Have spare balls spread around the outside for continuous, quick play.
- Make sure an extra attacking player is getting into Zone A or C quickly to support the attacking player as this is what you would want in a match.
- Quick forward passing where possible but also be patient and keep possession if required.
- If a player gives away possession too much from being lazy make them do 5 push ups quickly.

CHANGES/PROGRESSION:

- You can remove the 2 outside players if there are not enough numbers.
- Once play is flowing well and the players are engaged, make it so that if one team goes from Zone A to Zone C and back twice, the opposition do 10 push ups. This keeps the intensity up.

Starting shape: 1v1 in Zones A & C. 2v2 plus 3 overload players playing with the team in possession in Zone B. (Image: Session 1 - drill 2 - A)

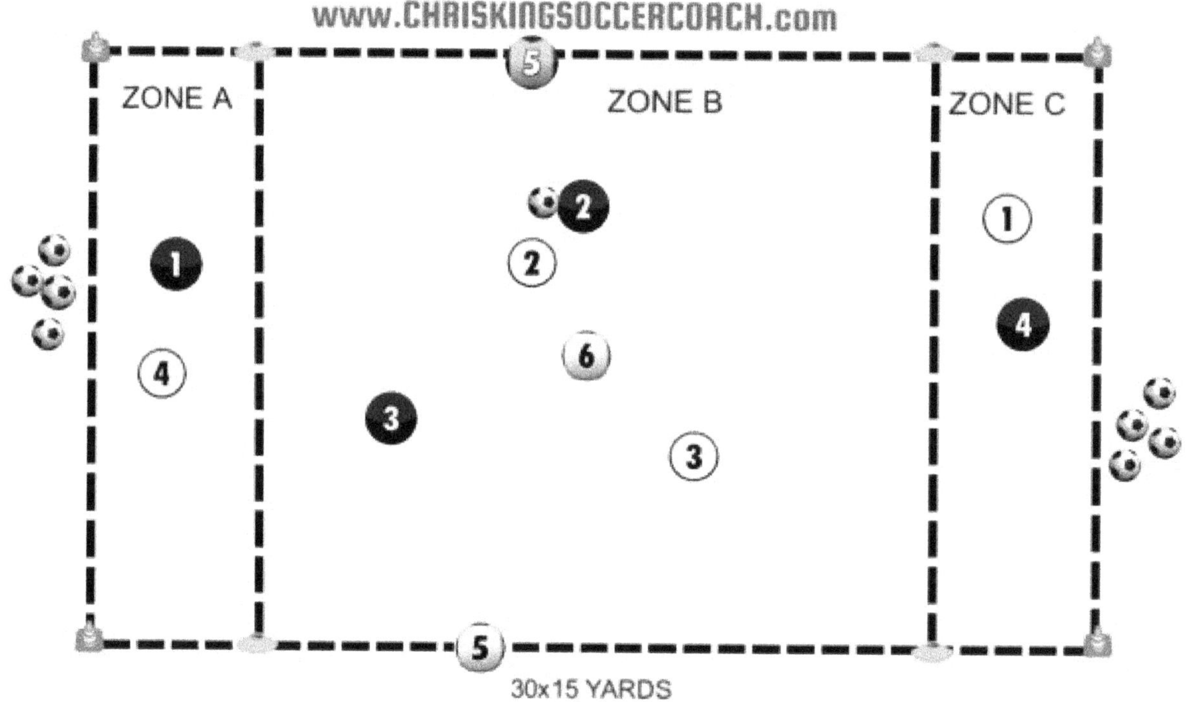

In play: When Black #2 passes into Black #1, Black #3 should enter Zone A to support. Once this is achieved, the Blacks try & move it back through the midfield (Zone B) and into Black #4 in Zone C. Always get an extra player in to support the players in Zone A & C before the ball can be played back out.

(Image: Session 1 - drill 2 - B)

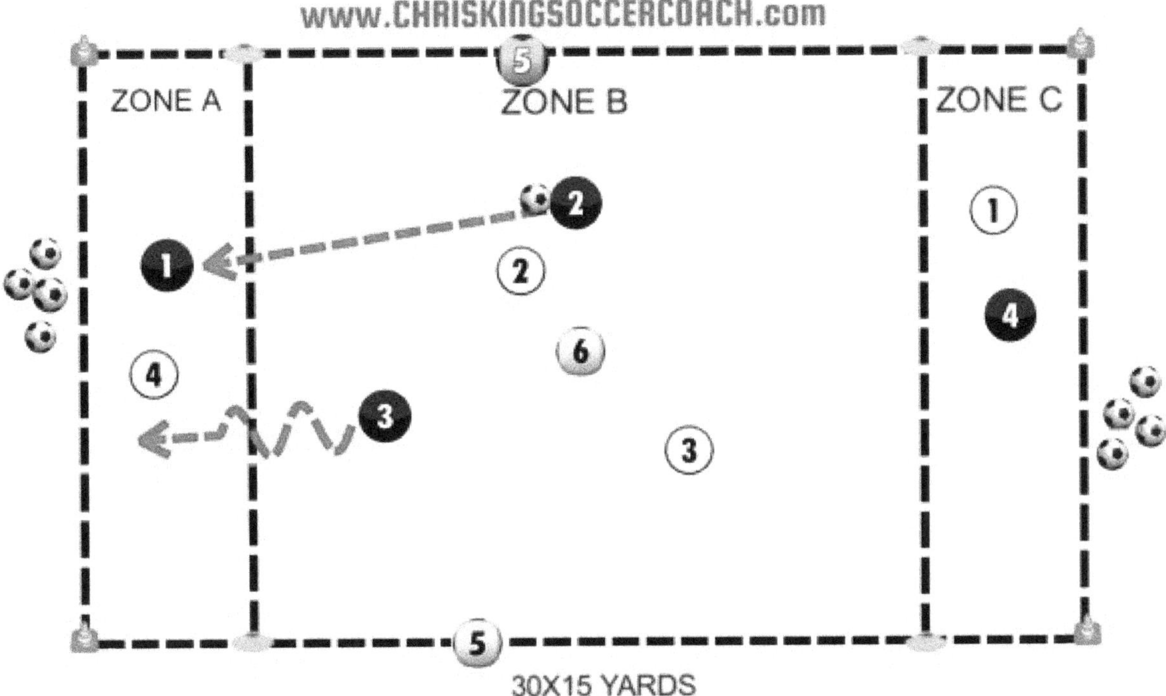

In play 2: In this example, Black #1 has received it and Black #3 has come in to support. Black #1 passes to Black #3 who passes back out to the overload player (#6) who uses the outside overload player (#5) who bounces it into Black #2 as they work it from one end to the other. (Image: Session 1 - drill 2 - C)

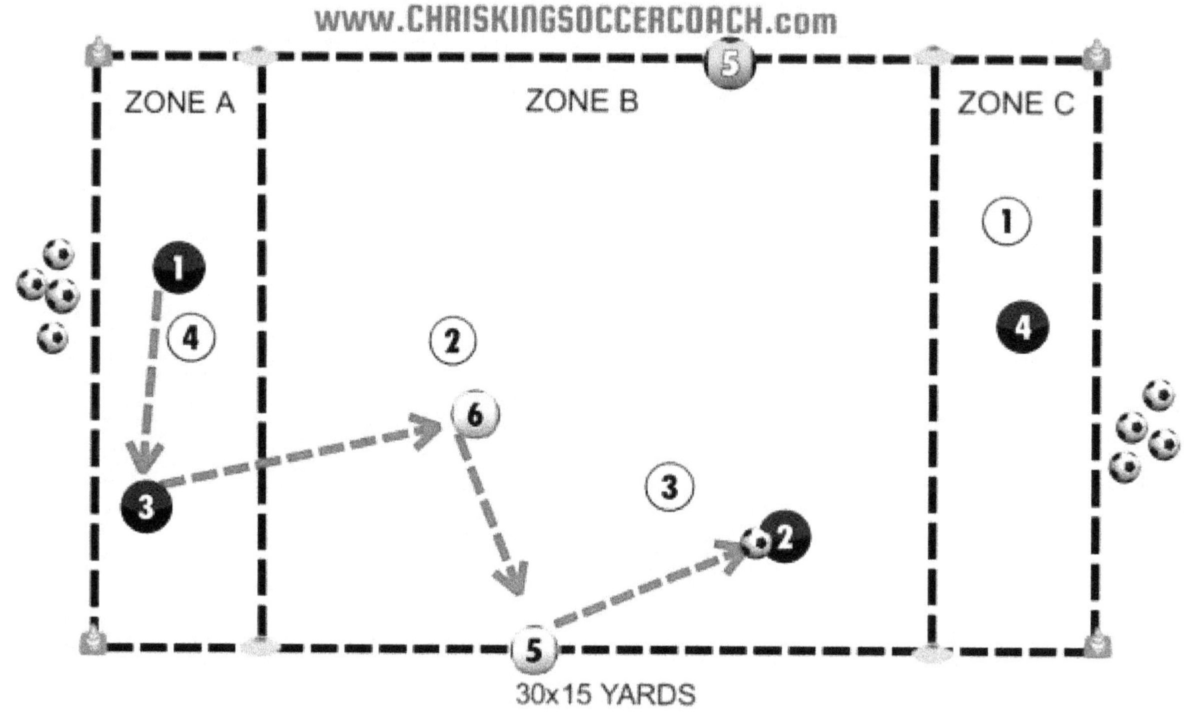

CHAPTER 5

SESSION 1 DRILL 3: COMBINATION PLAY TO SCORE GOALS (SMALL SIDED GAME)

PURPOSE:

- Overload the attacking areas to get intense, repetitive, quick fire shots on goals to give practice to both attacking players and goalkeepers.

SET UP:

- 11 Players (2 GK if available) (alternatively 9 or up to 14. Add or remove players as needed and adjust the size of the area accordingly.)
- 7 Cones
- 2 x medium goals (small or large if no medium)
- 25x40 yard area
- 20 minutes

THE DRILL:

- 2 teams of 4 with 3 Whites in one half v 1 Black, and 3 Blacks in the opposite half v 1 White.
- Overload player (#5) can play anywhere on the pitch with the team in possession.
- Teams look to combine from the GK in a 3+1v1 to shoot from within their own half. The player in the attacking half follows up for rebounds.
- If a goal is scored, that team keeps possession and play starts from their GK. If the shot is missed the opposition GK starts play.

KEY POINTS:

- Use depth, width and length.
- Expose the overload & use the spare player.

COACHES NOTES:

- Tell the GK's to be aware to start play quickly once a ball goes out (ie if a shot is missed the GK from that end quickly starts play. This encourages players to get in position quickly and to take advantage of other players who may have switched off).

- Have spare balls behind each goal.

- Push the players to do everything at pace.

- It will seem heavily overloaded (4v1+GK) to the team in possession when playing out but it is meant to be so the intensity is kept up and lots of shots are taken).

CHANGES:

- Challenge players individually (ie do things at pace; with 2 touches; move the ball to one side and shoot early).

- Limit touches to one or two.

PROGRESSION:

- The team in possession can play to their team mate in the attacking half to finish. Also, one player may dribble or pass across to the other half to shoot or combine with the attacking team mate in the attacking half.

Starting Shape: White attacking to the left, Blacks to the right.

3 defenders v 1 attacker in each half with an overload player (#5) playing with the team in possession. Play starts from the goalkeepers (or a coach from the outside if no goalies), if a team scores they keep possession and their goalkeeper restarts instantly. (Image: Session 1 - drill 3 - A)

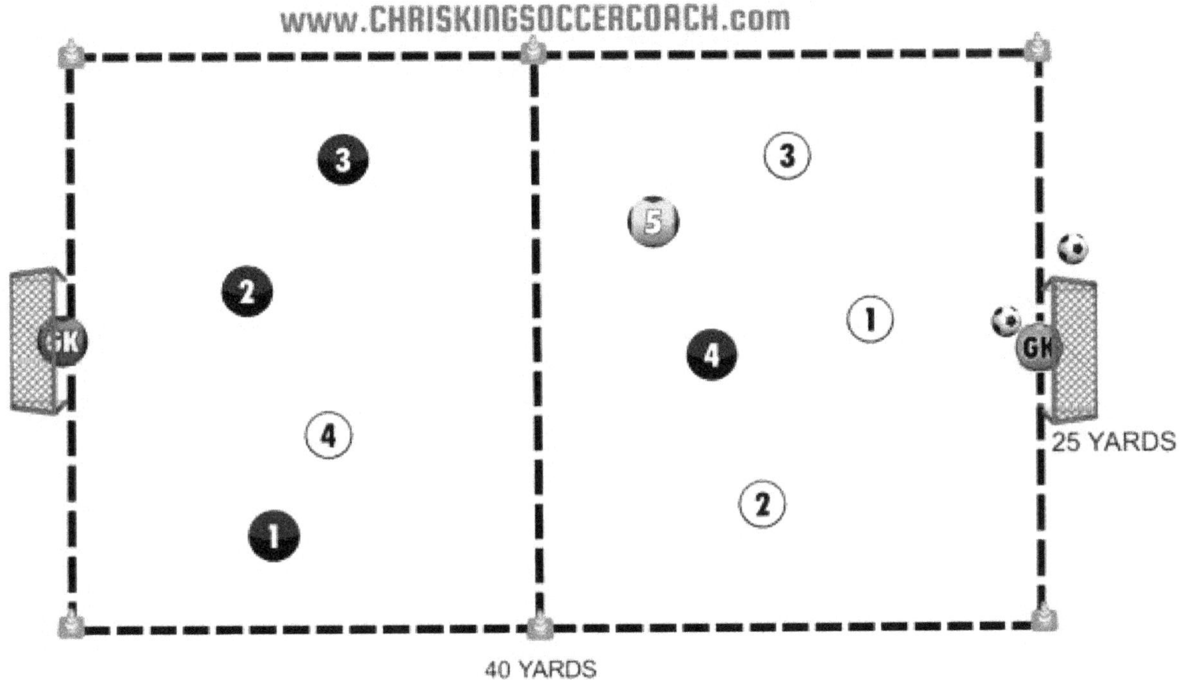

In Play: The player in possession (in this case #5) shoots & White #4 follows in for any rebounds. If there is a goal scored White keep possession & start from their GK again. (Image: Session 1 - drill 3 - B)

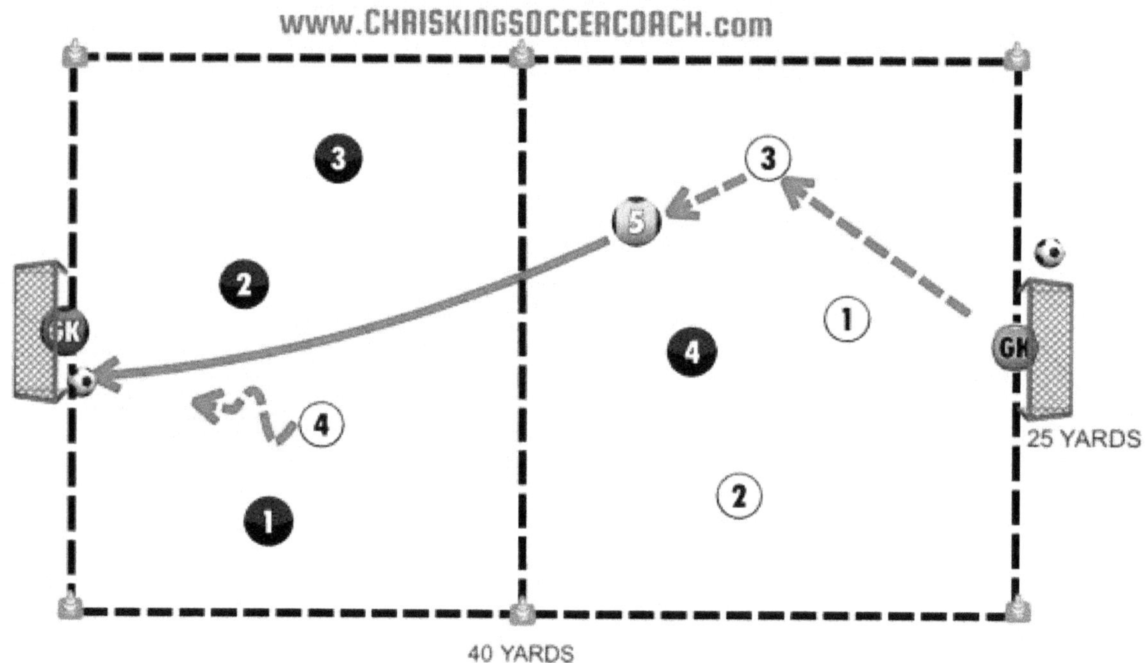

Progression: The player in possession (in this case #5) can either dribble into the other half and shoot, or pass to the forward (White #4) and enter that half and support them. This improves the players' decision making. (Image: Session 1 - drill 3 - C)

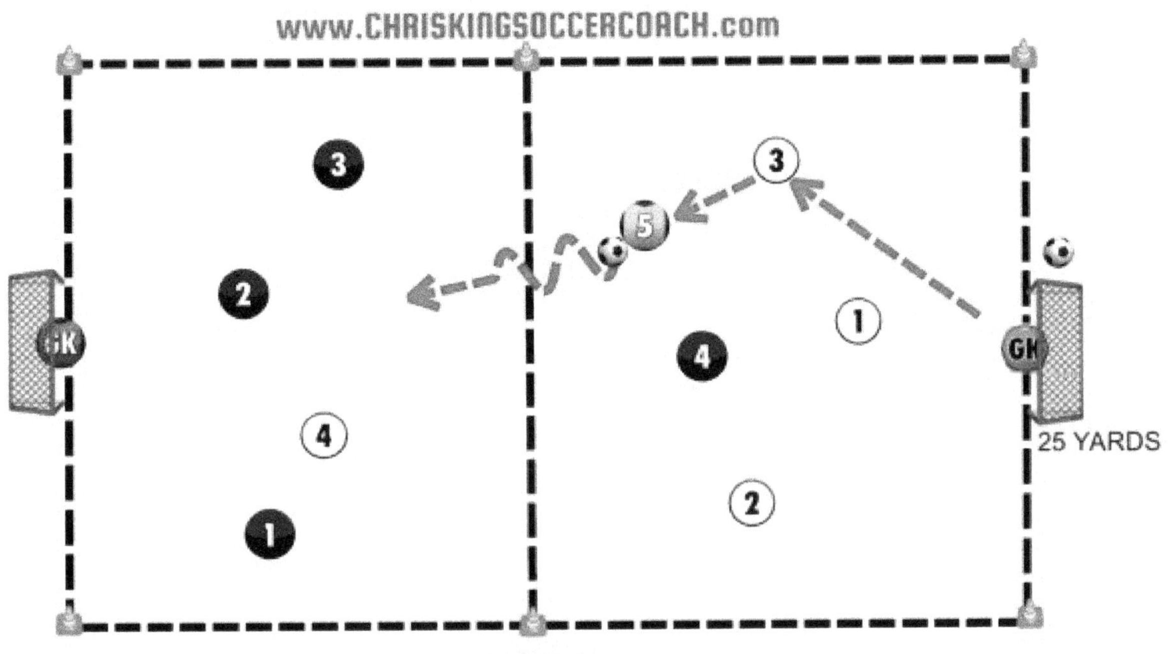

CHAPTER 6
SESSION 2: PRESSING

Parts of the players game that will be improved from this session:

Pressing; Positioning; Talking/organising team mates; Conditioning (fitness).

SESSION 2 DRILL 1: PRESSING RONDO

PURPOSE:

- Provide cover and balance with compact defending.
- Get used to using triggers to initiate the press.

SET UP:

- 9 Players (Alternatively 10,11,12 players - have 2 defensive players in each half; if 12, have one outside resting and swapping or collecting balls).

- 7 Cones

- 20x10 yard area

- 15 Minutes

THE DRILL:

- 6 Attacking players are positioned on the outside of the designated 10 yard lines of the area and 3 Defending players are inside the area. Only 2 defenders are allowed in a 10x10 grid at any one time (with the third one resting in the other 10x10 grid). The Defenders can rotate who goes in.

- The Attacking players aim to combine and play penetrative passes between the Defenders (this is called the 'third passing line') across the area without the Defenders intercepting the ball.

- Attackers must not go inside the area and must stay on the lines of the area or within a step either way.

- The Defenders aim to prevent the penetrative third line pass (don't get split in other words!) and look for opportunities to press and regain possession of the ball. They may tackle the Blacks.

- However, the Defenders should also look to prevent first line (left or right) and second line (forward left or forward right) passes, as these passes change the angle of attack.

- Once the Defenders have won possession or forced a misplaced pass on 3 occasions, change the 3 Defenders (or alternatively work for 2-3 minutes at a time to get conditioning).

COACHES NOTES:

- Get the defenders to communicate with each other all the time. "I'll press the ball", "I'm on your right" etc.

- Challenge the Defenders to win the ball back within 5 passes because in a match your best chance of winning the ball back is in the first few seconds.

- Defenders work hard in pairs to press but try not to get split by a pass.

- Defenders press hard when a trigger happens (ie Attacker has a bad touch or there is a slow pass).

CHANGES/PROGRESSION:

- Allow the 3 defenders to move anywhere inside the 20x10 area.
- Limit the players on the outside to 2 touches.
- Add an attacker (Black) into the middle who is free to move anywhere

Starting Shape: 6 Blacks v 3 Whites. 6 Blacks on each part of the rectangle passing to each other. 2 Whites working at once while the other rests.(Image: Session 2 - drill 1 - A)

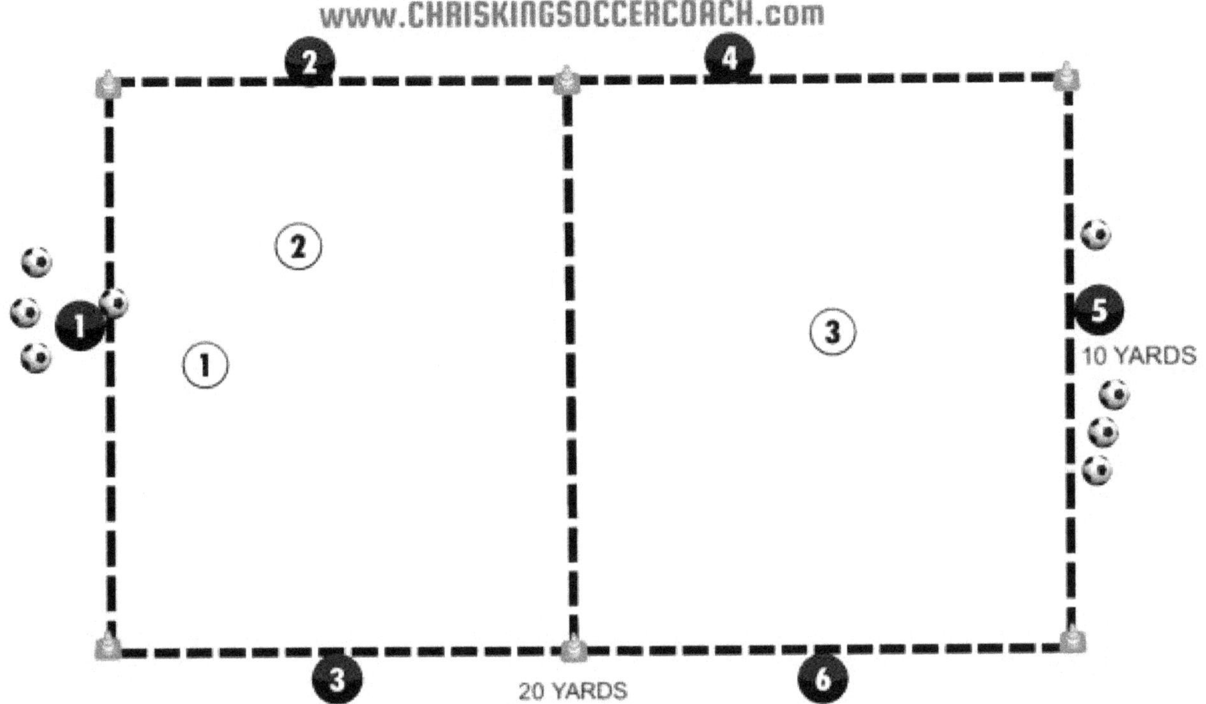

In Play: Black #1 passes to Black #2. Longer pass to Black #6 & White #2 moves to the other half to help White #3. (Image: Session 2 - drill 1 - B)

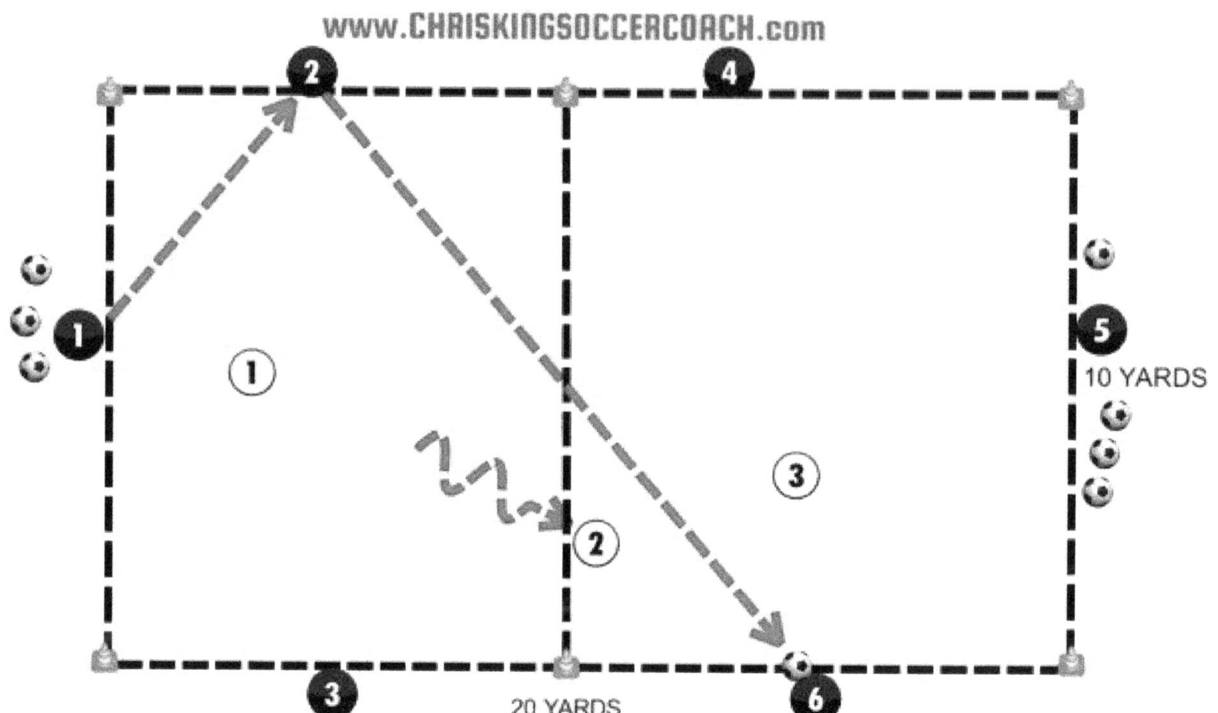

CHAPTER 7

SESSION 2 DRILL 2: PRESSURE POSSESSION GAME

PURPOSE:

- Press the ball carrier in high areas to try and win the ball. Improve conditioning & defensive organisation.

SET UP:

- 10 Players (alternatively 9,11,12,13 or 14. Have more players ready to come in at each end [or only 1 at each end if 9 players total]).
- 6 Cones
- 4 small goals
- 20x40 yard area
- 20 Minutes

THE DRILL:

- 4 attacking players (start with possession) v 3 defensive players.
- Play starts & restarts with either the coach passing a ball in to the attackers or the new fourth attacker bringing the ball in from their end.
- The attacking team of 4 must start behind the halfway point and get past halfway to score against 3 defenders in either of the small goals.
- Once the attackers have scored or the ball goes out, the highest positioned attacking player (from the 4 attackers) drops out and makes a recovery run around the ground to the back of their group, then a new players from the opposite team joins in on the ground and makes it a 4v3 in the opposite direction.
- If the defensive 3 wins the ball, they have 10 seconds to score.

KEY POINTS:

- Players aim to win the ball with pressure as high as possible.
- Players should prevent easy balls forward by blocking passing lanes.
- The closest player pressures the ball carrier to force them back or win the ball - the other players attempt to block passing lanes and set up in a small area of the ground defensively.
- If the defensive team wins the ball they can score (must do so within 10 seconds).

COACHES NOTES:

- It will take the players (and you!) a few run throughs to grasp this and to understand who comes in when. But stick with it, this is a great drill when it's running at full throttle. The key to this drill is lots of talking and every player (especially the ones waiting to come on) should be organising each other. Players should be telling each other who to push up on and who is blocking the passing lanes. Encourage them to organise each other. Once this drill is in full swing it should be very high intensity and players will get good fitness plus organising and pressing skills from it.

Starting Shape: Black team start (4 Blacks v 3 Whites). Blacks are attacking the goal to the right with a good structured build up. The White team presses the ball carrier and keeps a compact shape. As soon as a pass is made, the nearest White player should press high up on the ball carrier and the team mates should push up in the area of the pitch where the ball is and adjust as the ball moves.

(Image: Session 2 - drill 2 - A)

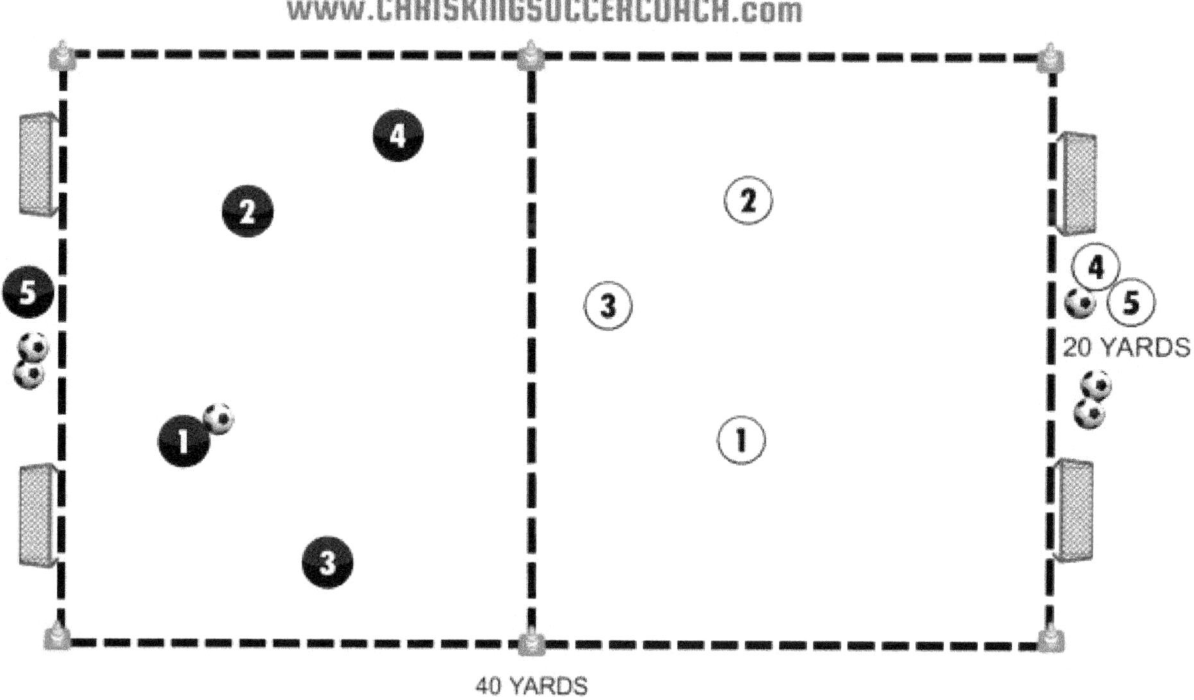

In Play 1: Once the Black team shoot, the highest Black player (Black #3 in this example) peels off and makes a recovery run around to the back of the line. At the same time, White #4 comes on with the ball and makes it 4 Whites v 3 Blacks and attack the goal to the left. If either team loses possession while in attack, the other team has 10 seconds to score.

(Image: Session 2 - drill 2 - B)

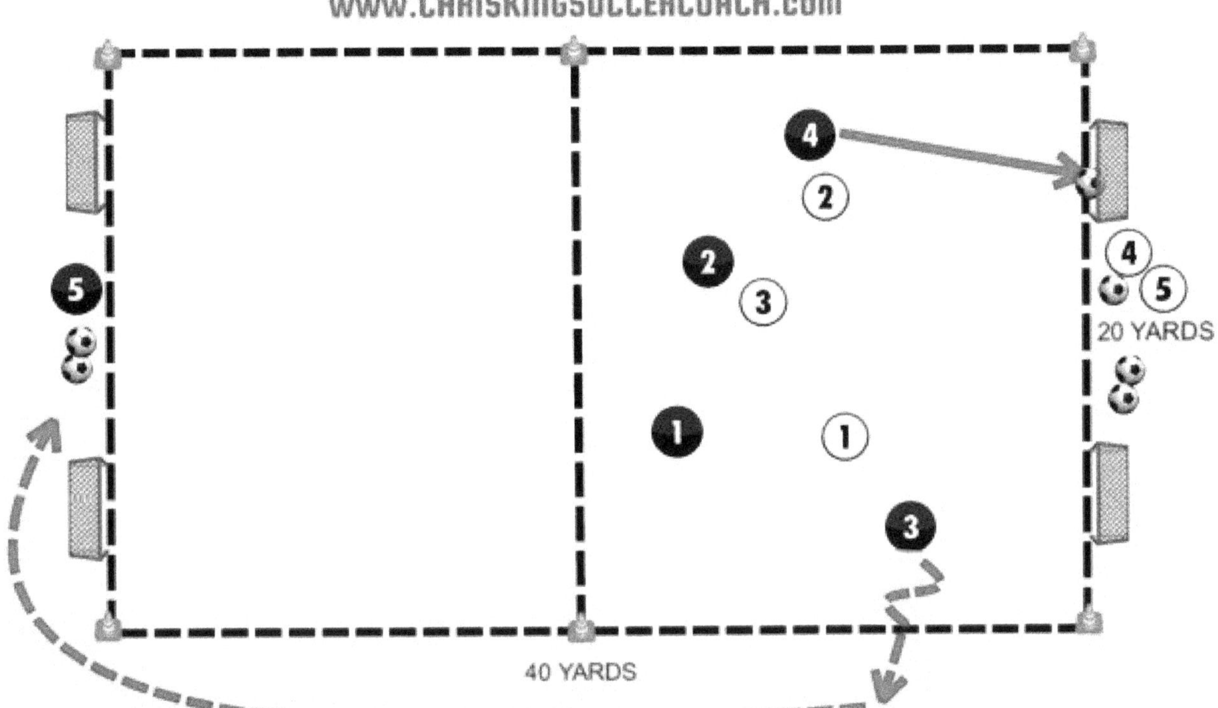
www.CHRISKINGSOCCERCOACH.com
20 YARDS
40 YARDS

In Play 2: Black team have just shot, the highest Black player (Black #3 in this example) is off the pitch. Now White #4 comes straight on to make it a 3 Black v 4 White situation and attack the goal to the left. Notice how Black #4 & #2 are shutting the ball carrier and Black #4 has made sure to block the passing lane so that White #4 can't easily pass to White #2.

(Image: Session 2 - drill 2 - C)

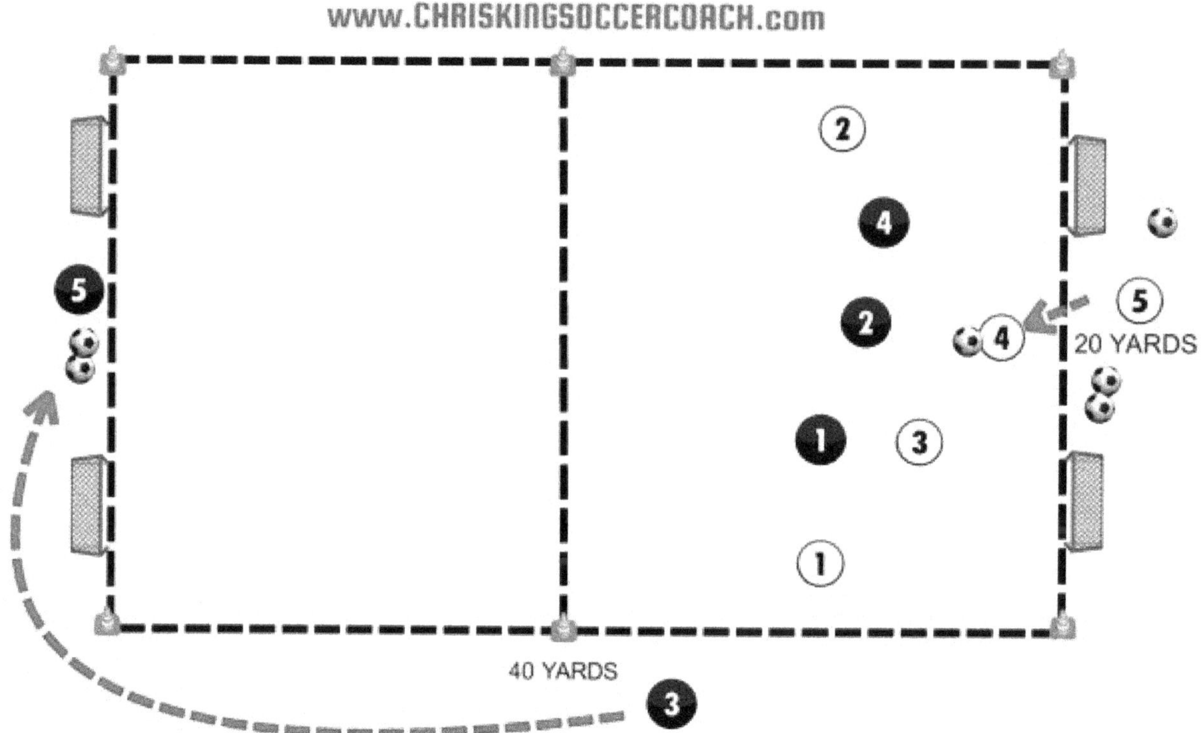

CHAPTER 8
SESSION 2 DRILL 3:
DEFENDING AS A UNIT AND PRESS FROM THE FRONT

PURPOSE:

- Work on forward press & playing through the press. Press from the front as a compact unit and alternatively play out from the back through the press.

SET UP:

- 18 Players (alternatively 12, 14 or 16 players [remove goalkeepers and/or 1 or 2 players from each midfield])

- 4 cones 2 discs

- 2 medium or large goals

- 30x50 yard area

- 20 Minutes

THE DRILL:

- 18 players (including 2 goalkeepers) are to set up as per the image. The 2 Full Backs (#1 & #4 from both teams in the image) are in their own half and must stay on the line in between their cones at all times (they can move along the line up to the half way but can not support past that. This makes attackers press).

- Defenders are to press the opposite players as a team with the objective of winning the ball back. Upon winning the ball back, players should look to counter attack quickly.

- When attacking, players should look to build from the back.

KEY POINTS:

- Compact defending.
- Use triggers so players know when to press.

COACHES NOTES:

- Use triggers (key moments in the game) to get your players to start the press. For example, if a slow pass is made, if a player has a bad touch or if their body shape is wrong, use these as triggers for the defensive team to press the opposition when they happen.

- Encourage the team in possession to build up from the back and to have faith in themselves.

Starting Shape: Black and White teams in a 4 1 3 formation. GK plays out to a centre back or full back and play is live. No long balls, encourage players to build up through good passing while under pressure from the press.

(Image: Session 2 - drill 3 - A)

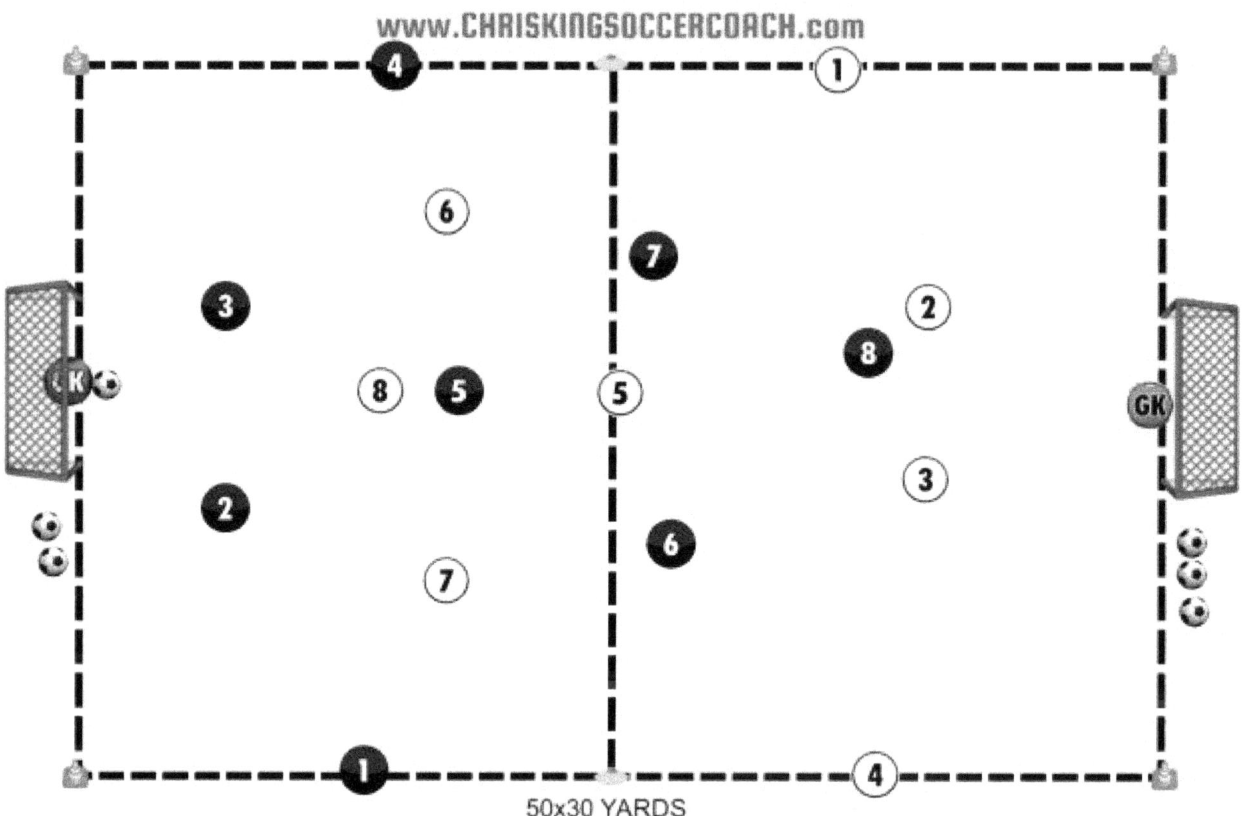

In Play: In this instance, the GK has played a ball to a centre back facing their own goal (Black #3). This is a trigger for the White team to press!

White #8 presses the ball carrier (Black #3), White #6 moves over to block the passing lane to Black #7 and is also in a position where he can quickly get to Black #4. White#7 pushes across to cut out the option to Black #2 and the rest of the White team push up. This blocks off options and also importantly creates numbers further up the pitch so if they do get a turn over from the press they can use their numerical advantage and attack.

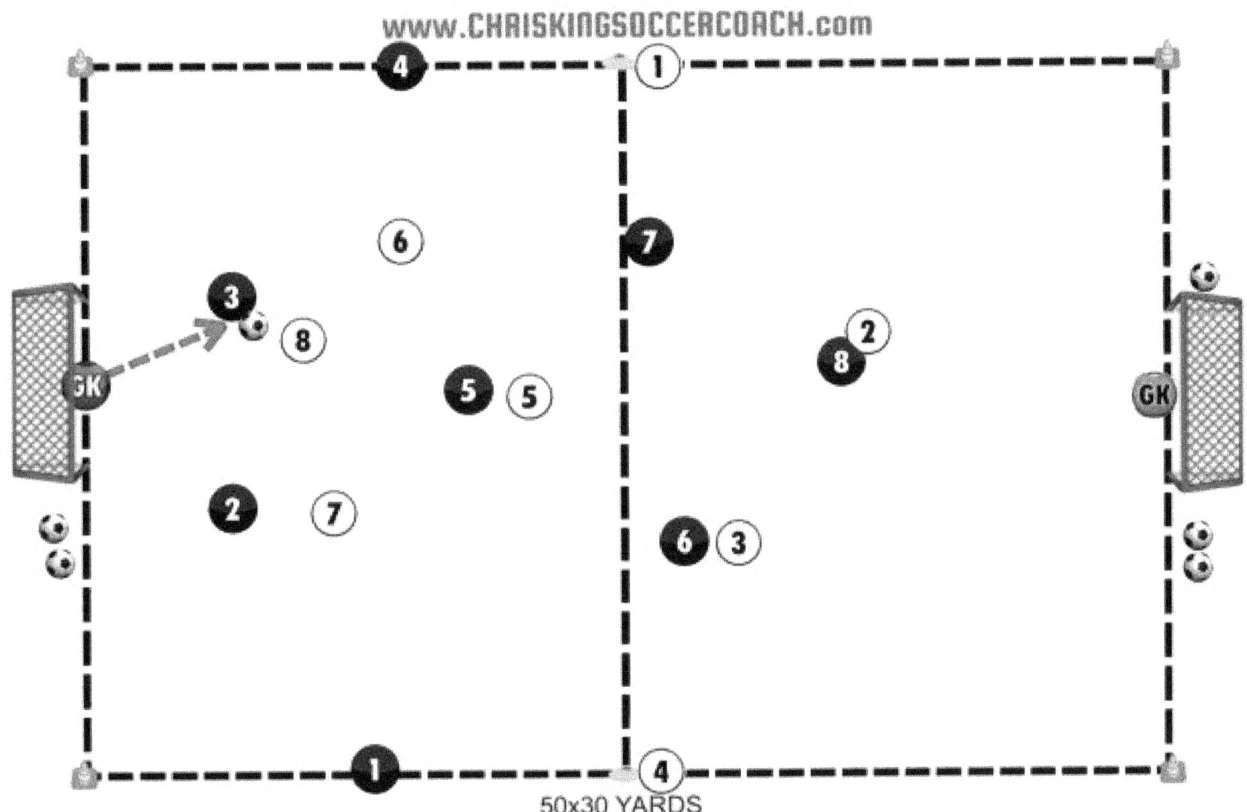

CHAPTER 9

SESSION 3: MIDFIELD PLAY - FINDING SPACE BETWEEN LINES

Parts of the players game that will be improved from this session:

Midfield positioning and awareness; Midfielders decision making on when to pass or dribble.

SESSION 3 DRILL 1:
WHEN TO DRIBBLE, WHEN TO PASS RONDO

PURPOSE:

- For midfielders to gain confidence and awareness of when to dribble or when to pass.

SET UP:

- 6 Players (alternatively 7 or 8 players: make the square into a circle and spread the attackers evenly around. Don't make the circle too large as there are only 2 defenders.

- 4 Cones

- 10x10 yard area

- 15 Minutes

THE DRILL:

- Players pass between themselves on the outside, moving the defenders around and trying to pass between them when possible. At any time, players can dribble to another line but there must be another player switching to that vacated line (this is key as we are teaching players to make the decision of when to pass or dribble. So encourage them to mix it up based on if there is time or space to dribble or not).

- If the outside players pass between the two defenders (split them) they get one point. If a player successfully dribbles to another line it's one point.

- If the Whites win the ball, they must keep it and one Black (whoever made the mistake) enters the area and tries to win the ball back. If the Whites make 5 passes they get one point and keep passing between themselves until Black wins it back.

- Players are to work as defenders for 90 seconds, then rotate.

- Add up the points and the losers do 10 push ups. Hard, short, sharp work.

COACHES NOTES:

- Get all the players to talk!
- Work on players' decision making on when to pass or dribble.

CHANGES/PROGRESSION:

- Make the area smaller.
- One touch for the outside players.

Starting Shape: 4 Blacks v 2 Whites. Blacks can pass or dribble to any line but another Black must change places if they dribble to their line. Whites press together trying to win the ball and trying not to get split by the pass. (Image: Session 3 - drill 1)

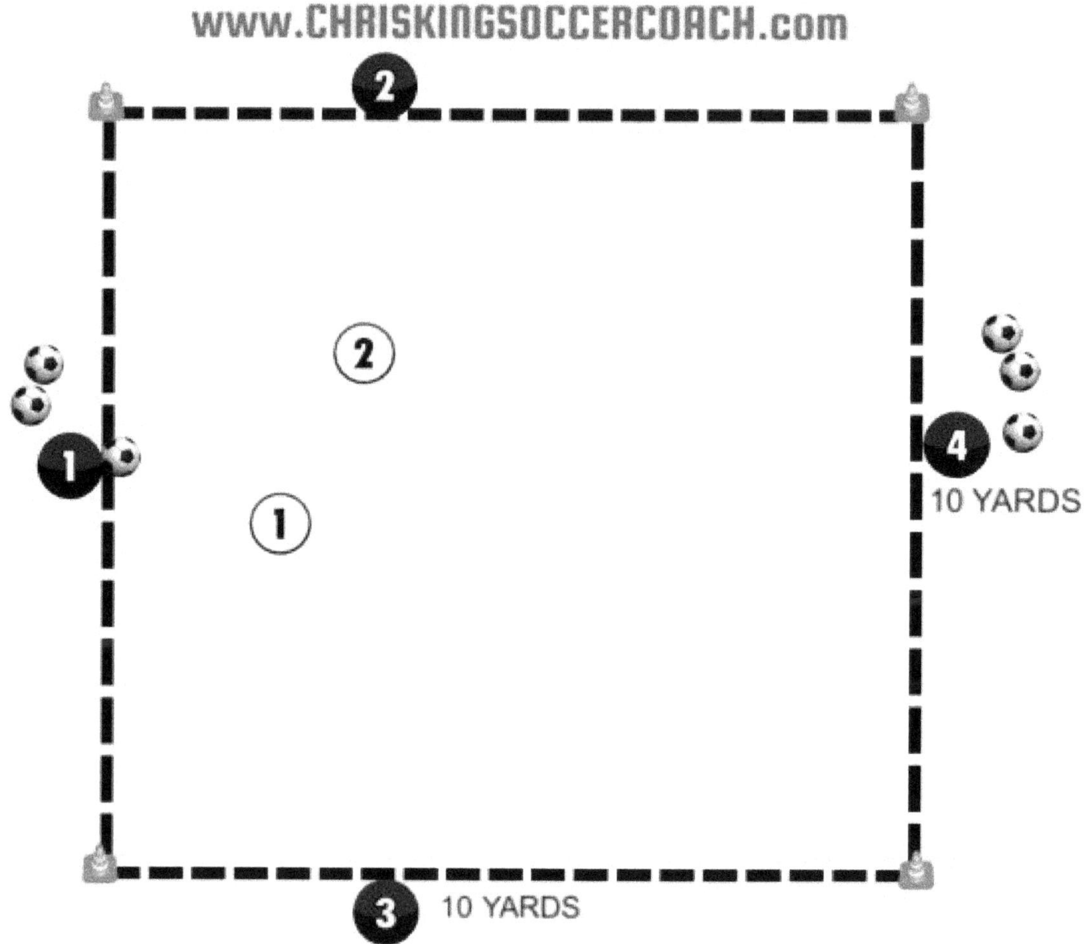

In Play: Black #1 passes to Black #2. Black #2's pass is intercepted by White #2.

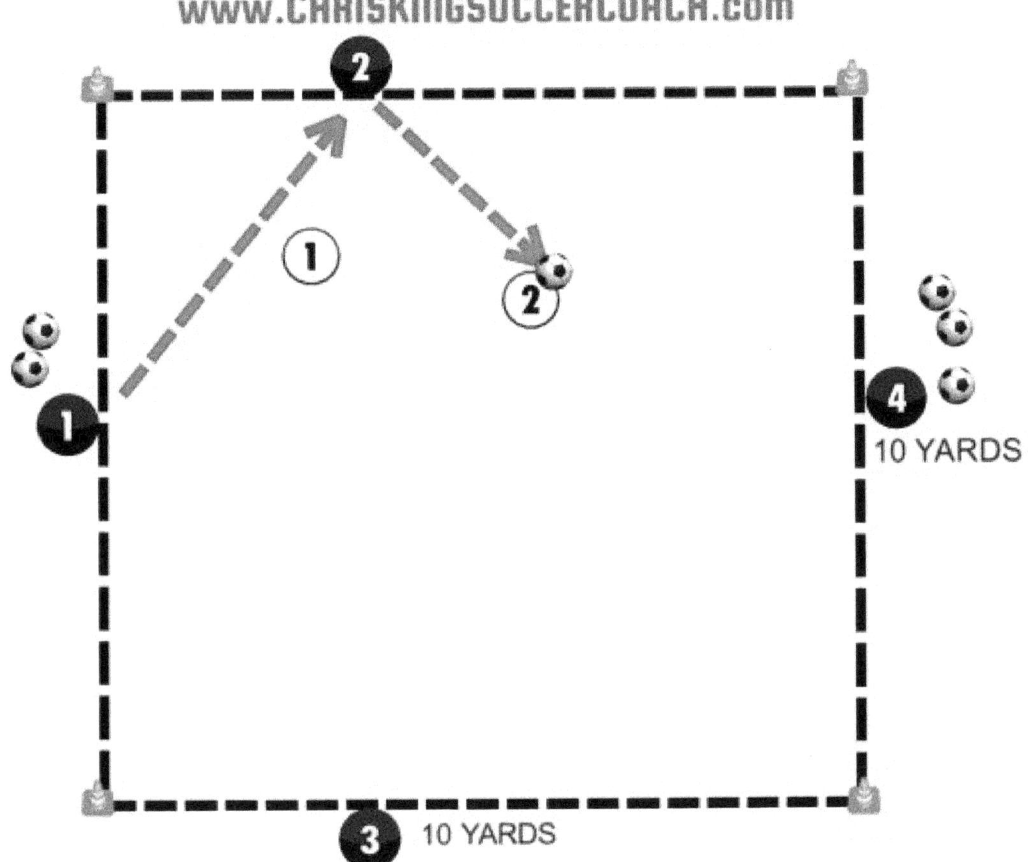

In Play 2: Black #2 must now try and win the ball back while White #1 & #2 keep it off him. Play restarts when Black #2 wins back possession.

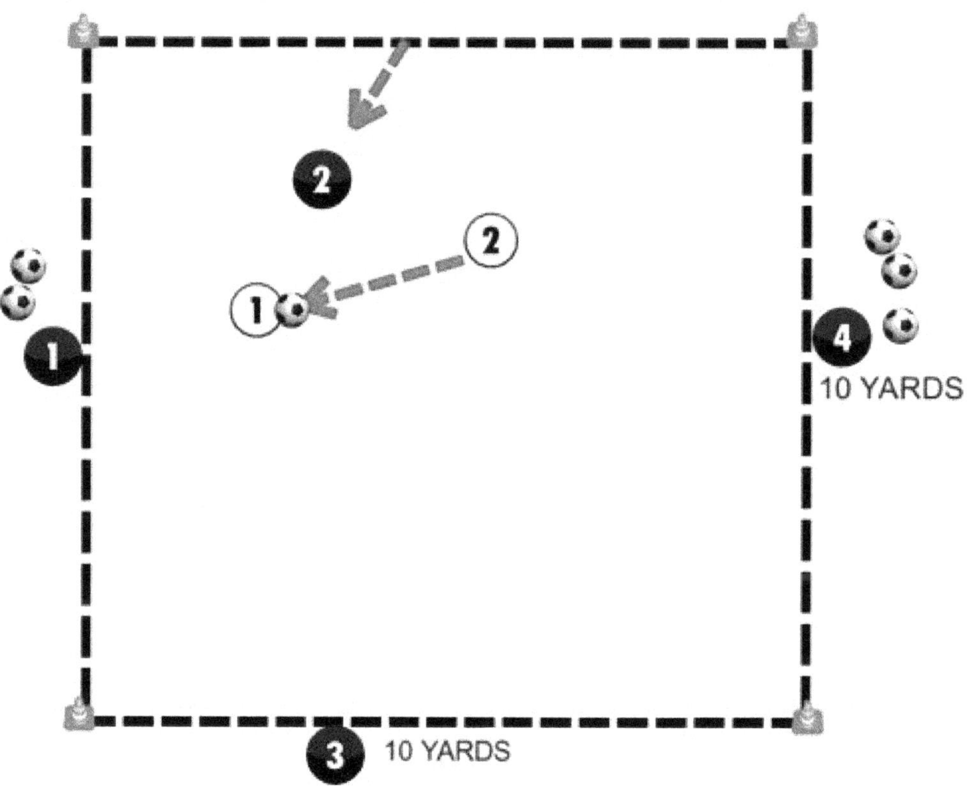

CHAPTER 10

SESSION 3 DRILL 2: FINDING SPACE BETWEEN THE LINES

PURPOSE:

- This drill will introduce the idea of finding space in between the lines (meaning, for example, finding the space between the oppositions defensive line and midfield line. This is important as in these areas you can receive the ball unopposed. Plus it creates confusion for the opposition defenders as they are unsure whether they should be marking you or not).

SET UP:

- 8 Players (alternatively 7 or 10 players: take out Black #5 and the coach acts as that player or put a small goal there instead. Or for 10 players, add another defender and midfield in the area)

- 10 Concs

- 20x10 yard area

- 15 Minutes

THE DRILL:

- There is a 5x10 yard 'channel' set up in the middle to replicate the area in a match that would be 'playing in between the lines'.

- There are 5 Attackers (Black) in possession and play always starts with the Centre Back (Black #1) on the end line.

- 3 Defenders (White) in the central area to prevent the Black team playing from Centre Backs (Black #1) to Centre Forward (Black #5).

- There are 3 Defenders (White) in the centre. White #1 & White #2 in one half, White #3 in the other half. White are not allowed in the middle channel!

- Centre Back (Black #1), Full Backs (Black #2 & Black #4) and Centre Forward (Black #5) can move along their designated lines only. Centre Midfielder (Black #3) can move anywhere in the square including the central (yellow) zone. However, they can only stay in the zone for a maximum of 3 seconds and have a maximum of 2 touches (change this depending on the age and ability of your players).

- Once Black #5 has received the ball, play restarts from Black #1.

KEY POINTS:
Coordinated movements of the players.
Quality of the pass.
COACHES NOTES:

- Get the Black #3 to be constantly 'head checking' to see where she is in relation to the defenders and what her options to pass to are. This is a key point for a midfielder, they should know ahead of receiving the ball what their options are.

- The Black #3 can work anywhere in the area but she should be trying to get in between the lines in the centre channel, especially when the fullbacks (Black #2 & #4) have possession.

- Make sure to get the fullbacks (Black #2 & #4) to work up and down their lines to support.

- Get the two Whites to work together and block passing lanes where possible.

CHANGES/PROGRESSION:
Make it harder:

- Challenge the players individually.
- Make the areas smaller.
- Take out the zone.
- Limit touches.
- Add defenders.

Starting Shape: 4 Blacks on the outside lines working up and down their lines. Black #1 acting as the centre back playing it out to his fullbacks (Black #2 or #4) or to his deep midfielder (Black #3). (Image: Session 3 - drill 2 - A)

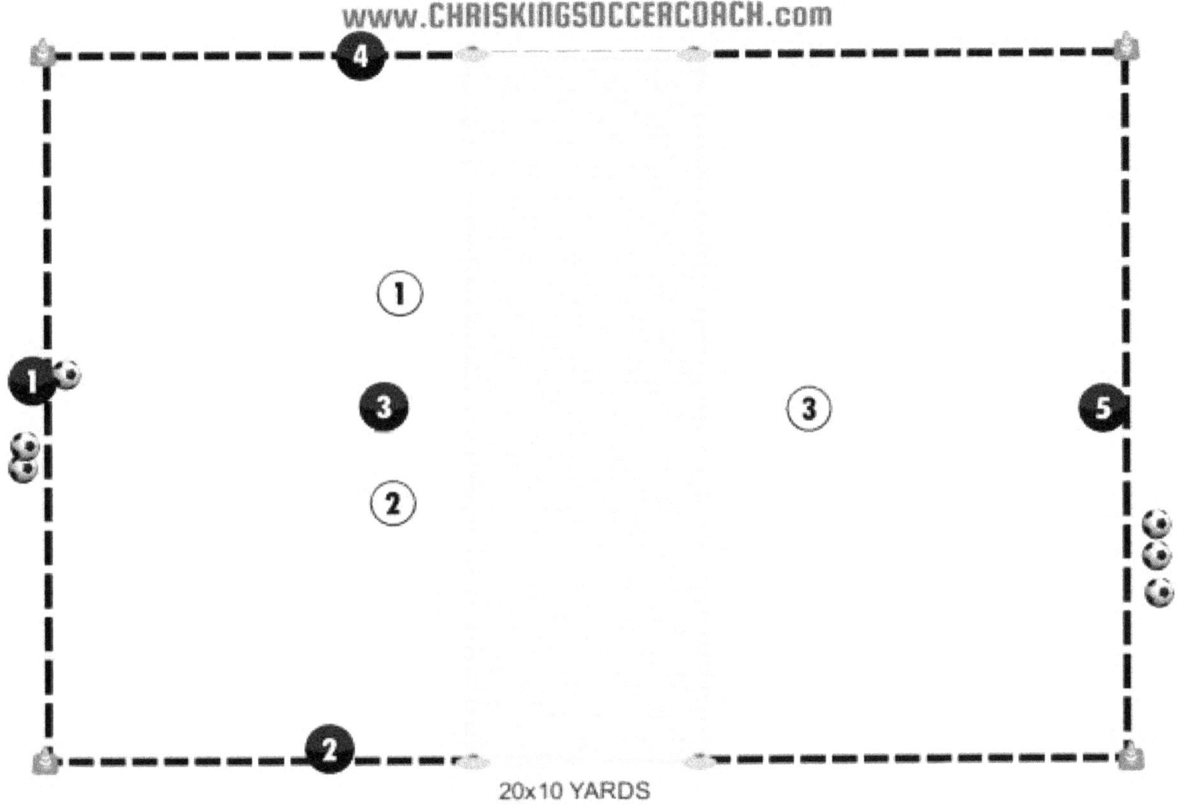

In Play: In this example, Black #1 has passed to Blue #4. Black #3 moves in between the lines of the opposition so she can receive it from Black #4. At the same time Black #2 and Black #5 have moved into positions where they can support or receive the ball.

(Image: Session 3 - drill 2 - B)

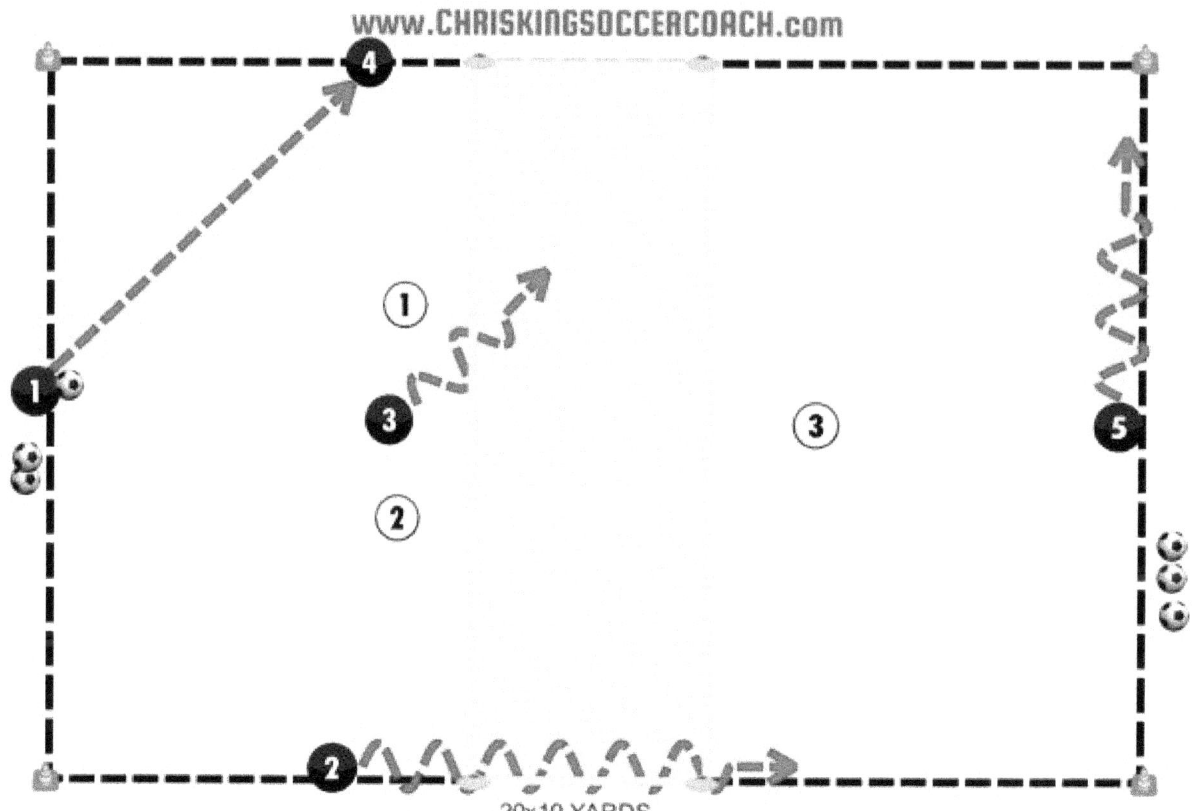

CHAPTER 11

SESSION 3 DRILL 3: MIDFIELD PLAY - PLAYING FORWARD

PURPOSE:

- For midfielders to work on their formation and play forward at every opportunity.

SET UP:

- 18 Players (alternatively 14 to 22 players. When adding or removing players, take them from Zones A & C first).
- 8 Cones
- 30x50 yard area
- 20 Minutes

THE DRILL:

- Players are to stay in each third as per the diagram.
- Play through the three thirds of the pitch (no long hopeful balls from Zone A to Zone C, make sure to get the players to build through the midfield in Zone B).

KEY POINTS:

- Play forward where possible! Get the player's body shape facing forward where possible.
- Good first touch on the ball so the players can move it quickly.

COACHES NOTES:

The points below should be communicated to the midfield in Zone B from both teams:

- When in possession of the ball you need to be in 2-1 or 1-2 shape (we don't want all three side by side)
- Allow yourself to get into a position where you can see your other midfielders (constantly head check to get awareness of opposition and team mates).
- Drop the shoulder to deceive your opponent so you can get space to receive the ball. And also drop off the shoulder of your opposition player so they lose track of you and you get in their blind spot.
- Attempt to play forward where possible.

Starting Shape: Blacks attacking left to right. Both teams set up with 3 defensive players (#1,2,3), 3 midfielders (#4,5,6) and 2 attackers (#7,8) plus goalkeepers. If you have less or more numbers take a defender out or add a defender in for each team.

(Image: Session 3 - drill 3)

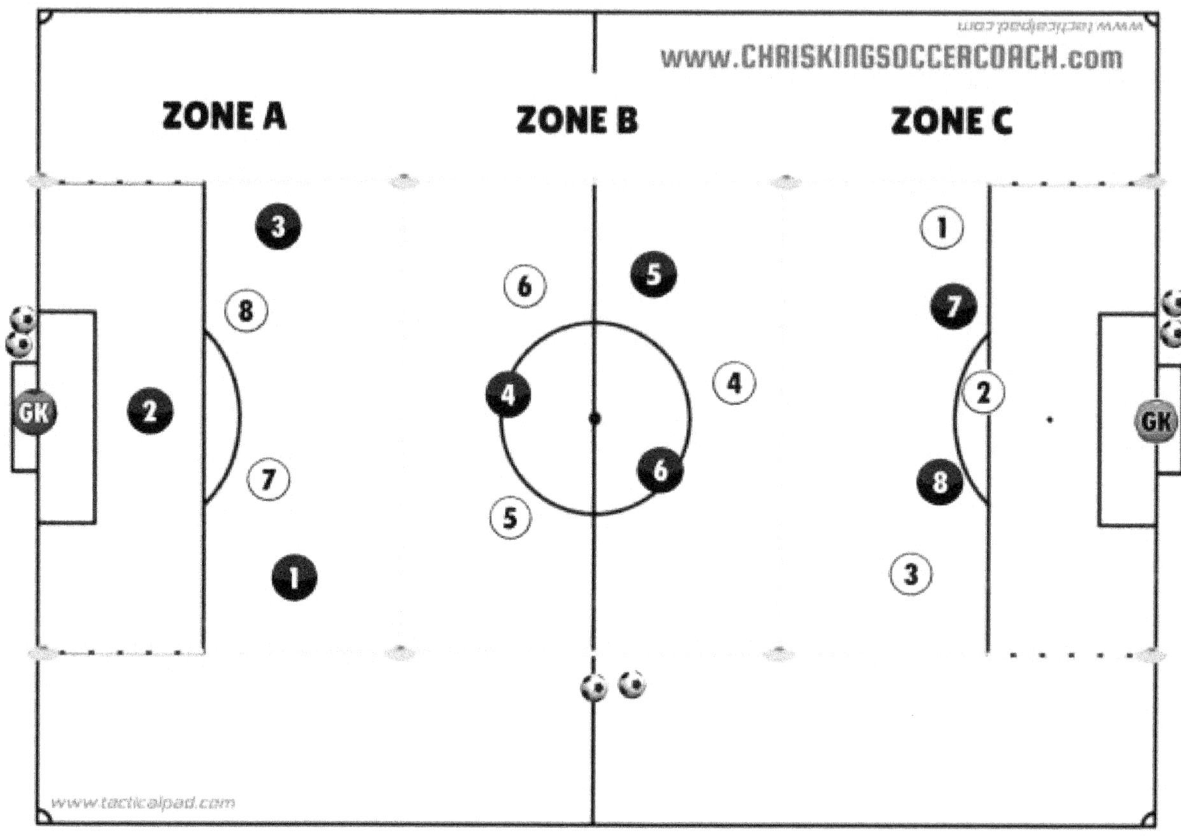

CHAPTER 12
SESSION 4: PLAYING OUT FROM THE BACK

Parts of the players game that will be improved from this session:

Defensive positioning; Playing out from the back under pressure.

SESSION 4 DRILL 1:
BACK FOUR DEFENDING POSSESSION GAME

PURPOSE:

- For defenders to gain confidence and awareness of when to play out from the back. Keeping a defensive shape.

SET UP:

- 12 Players (alternatively 9 or 15 players - with 9 players, take one out of each team and play in a back three formation with one centre back and two full backs. With 15 players add one to each team and make the area larger and play with a player in front of the back four)

- 4 Cones 6 discs

- 40x15 yard area

- 15 Minutes

THE DRILL:

- The team in the middle is defending. The team with the ball (Black) attempts to play through the middle section and get the ball to the White team. If successful the White team maintains possession and attempts to play the ball back through the middle section to the Black team.

- The middle defensive team (#5,6,7,8) aim to keep a good zonal defending shape (they move across as the ball moves) and aim to intercept the pass.

- After 3 minutes (or the middle team wins it 5 times) swap defenders.

KEY POINTS:

- The focus is on the middle third defensive team, in which the aim is to maintain good defensive zonal shape (Zonal: means moving to the area where it is best for the team. As opposed to man marking where all the players follow their man).

COACHES NOTES:

- The closest player goes toward the ball and the other 3 set up a curve shape (horse shoe) to cut out the passing lanes. The furthest defender away provides balance.

- If the ball gets switched to the other side, the back 4 then shuffle across, maintaining that shape.

- If the ball goes back centrally, the closest player goes towards the ball and the other defenders step up and maintain their shape to ensure there are no gaps.

CHANGES/PROGRESSION:

- After each team goes through once, the progression is that one player from the defensive middle can go into the attacking team square to make it a 4v1 and the remaining three maintain good zonal defensive shape.
- Provide competition - if a middle team gets the ball passed through them 3 times in a row give them a punishment.

Starting Shape: Blacks try to pass it through to Whites while the middle team (#5,6,7,8) keep a good zonal defensive shape. Notice how Middle #5 has pushed towards the ball carrier (Black #2) and the other 3 Middle defenders have pushed across to where the ball is and keep a good curved shape to block passing lanes. (Session 4 - drill 1 - A)

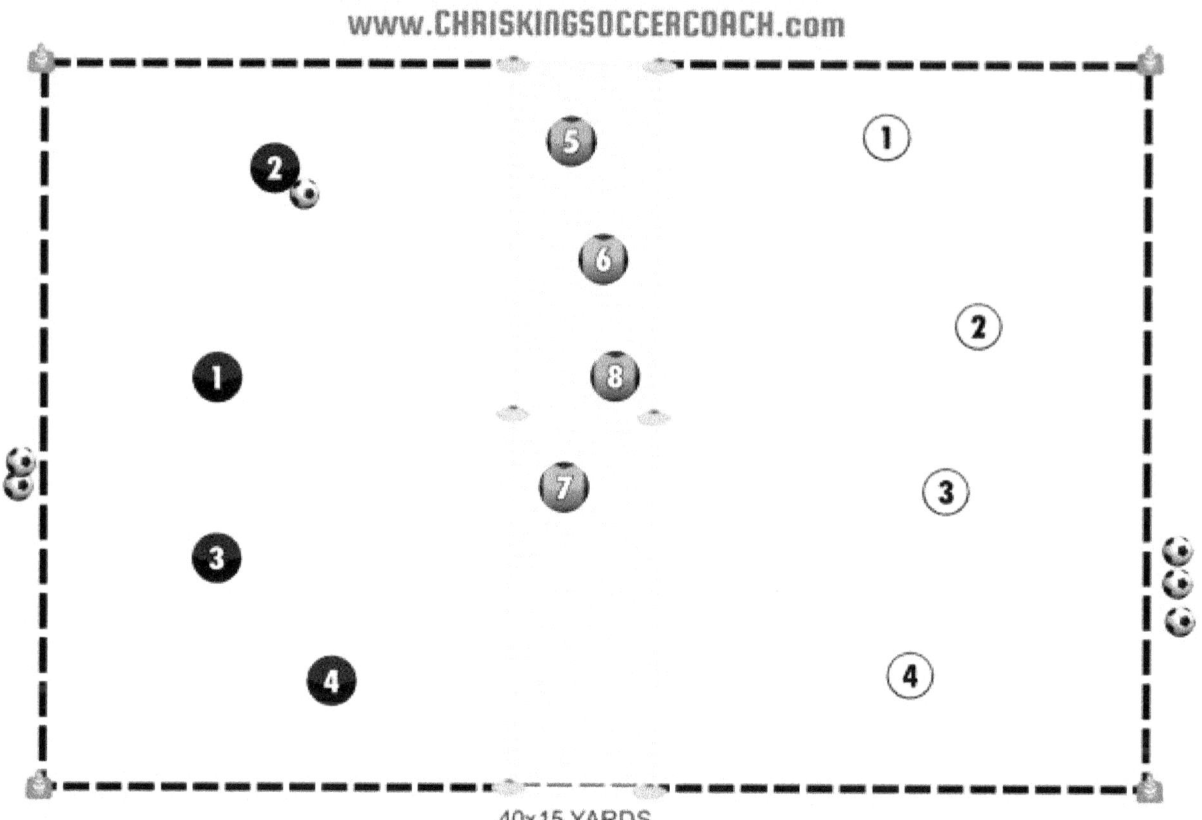

In Play: Black #2 passes to Black #1 who in turn passes to Black #4. The Middle defenders have moved across in a good defensive shape but were slightly slow so Black #4 was able to pass it through to White #4.

If the ball was to next pass from White #4 to White #3, Middle #8 should move forward towards White #3 (stay in the channel still) & the other players should keep their shape & block any passing lanes.

(Image: Session 4 - drill 1 - B)

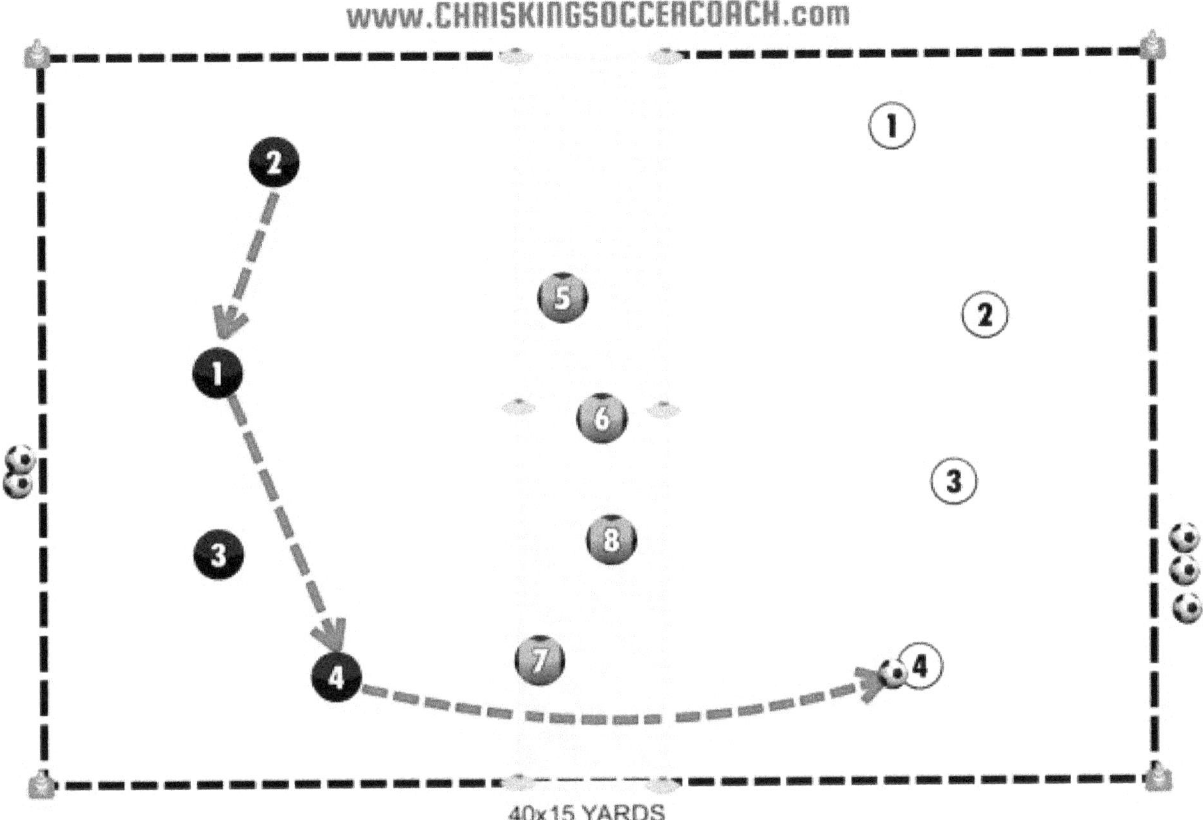

Progression: A Middle player (#8) can now push into the area where the ball is and try and win possession (towards White #4). The other 3 Middle defenders keep a good, tight, defensive shape and aim to continue to block passing lanes.

(Image: Session 4 - drill 1 - C)

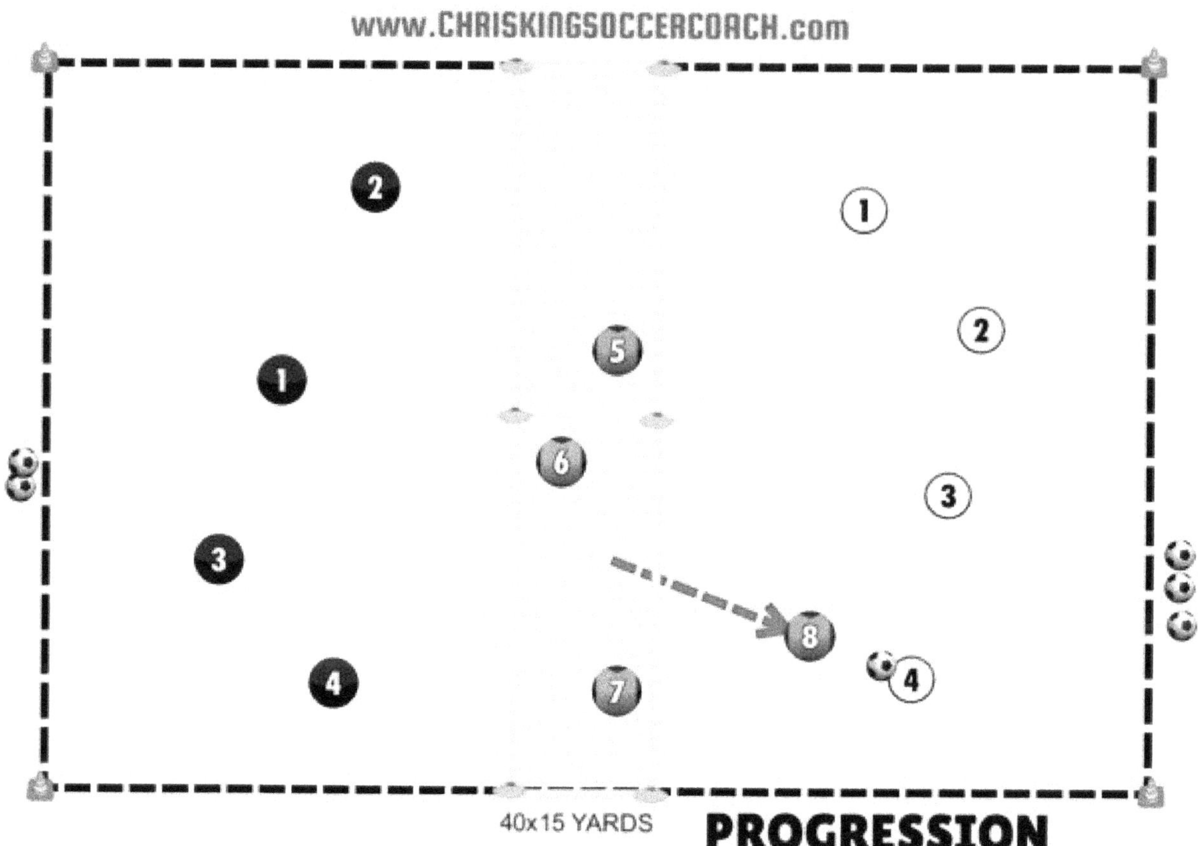

CHAPTER 13
SESSION 4 DRILL 2:
PLAYING OUT FROM THE BACK
(COMBINATIONS TO PLAY INTO THE MIDDLE THIRD)

PURPOSE:

- Improve defensive players ability to play out from the back and into the midfield.

SET UP:

- 11 Players (alternatively 9 or 13 players. Either take a player out from each team and play as a back three or add a player to each team and have a midfielder on both teams. Goalkeepers or the coach can be used as the bouncers [#1] if you wish)

- 4 Cones

- 20x25 yard area

- 20 Minutes

THE DRILL:

- The end bouncer plays out to the Black team who then combine with the Overload player (#6), making it a 6v5, and try to play the ball through to the bouncer at the other end ('bouncer' is so called in these drills as they are used to play the ball off but aren't allowed in the area).

- If successful in getting the ball from one end to the other, play instantly restarts from the other end (ie the team that got it from one end to the other is rewarded by getting to keep possession & starts again). The #1 can be used as you would use a goalkeeper in a game when playing out from the back.

- If the defensive team wins the ball back, they play back to their team's bouncer and then play continues.

- To summarise the above points: Black #1 & White #1 are playing on both teams. Black try to get it through to the White #1, if successful play restarts from Black #1 straight away. White do the opposite. The Overload player (#6) plays on the team in possession.

KEY POINTS:

- Body shape of the receiving player is to go forward - so they should be side on and receive the ball on their furthest foot away to go forward.

- Drop off the shoulder of the defensive opponent (i.e. peel off so you're in the blind spot of the defender and in space).

- Maintain possession - if they can't go forward come back and switch play out to the other side.

- Overload player (#6) is to provide support wide and in the middle.

COACHES NOTES:

Make sure the players get into theses shapes:

- ***In Possession:*** When the bouncer (#1) has the ball, get into a typical back 4 shape - left and right players (#2 & #5) get high and wide and the deeper players (#3 & #4) split and middle player (#6) stays central.

- ***Not in possession:*** Allow the pass to go out to one side and then tuck in and push over that side to reduce the space. The closest player presses the ball, mimicking Drill 1.

Starting Shape: Black (in possession) are in a good back four shape. The full backs are high and wide, the centre backs are split so the opposition have to choose who to mark and can't cover both at once. (Image: Session 4 - drill 2 - A)

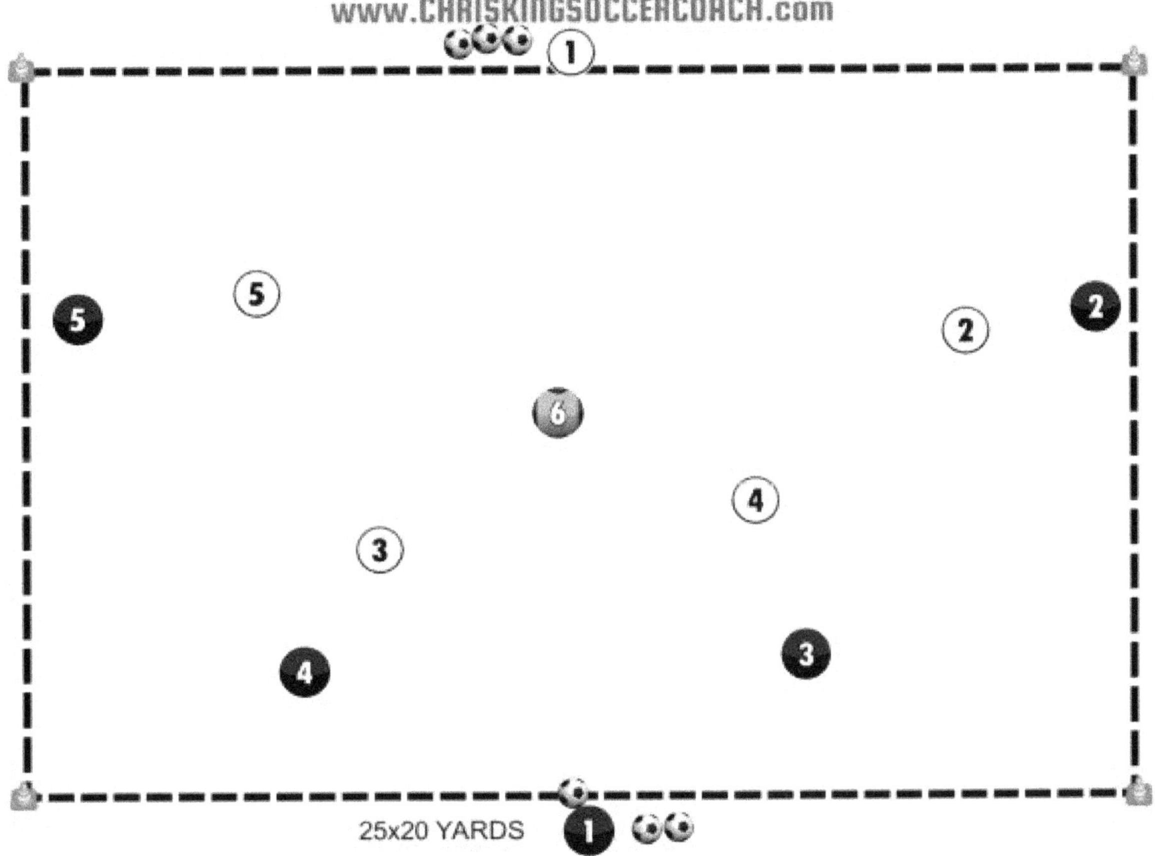

In Play: Black have played it out from #1 to #4 to #5, to the overload player (#6) and into White #1 (this player in a real match would be an attacking midfielder or striker). White #1 leaves the ball and play immediately starts again from Black #1.

If White had won possession, they play it to their White #1, quickly get in their back four formation (like Black were) and play continues with White in possession.

(Image: Session 4 - drill 2 - B)

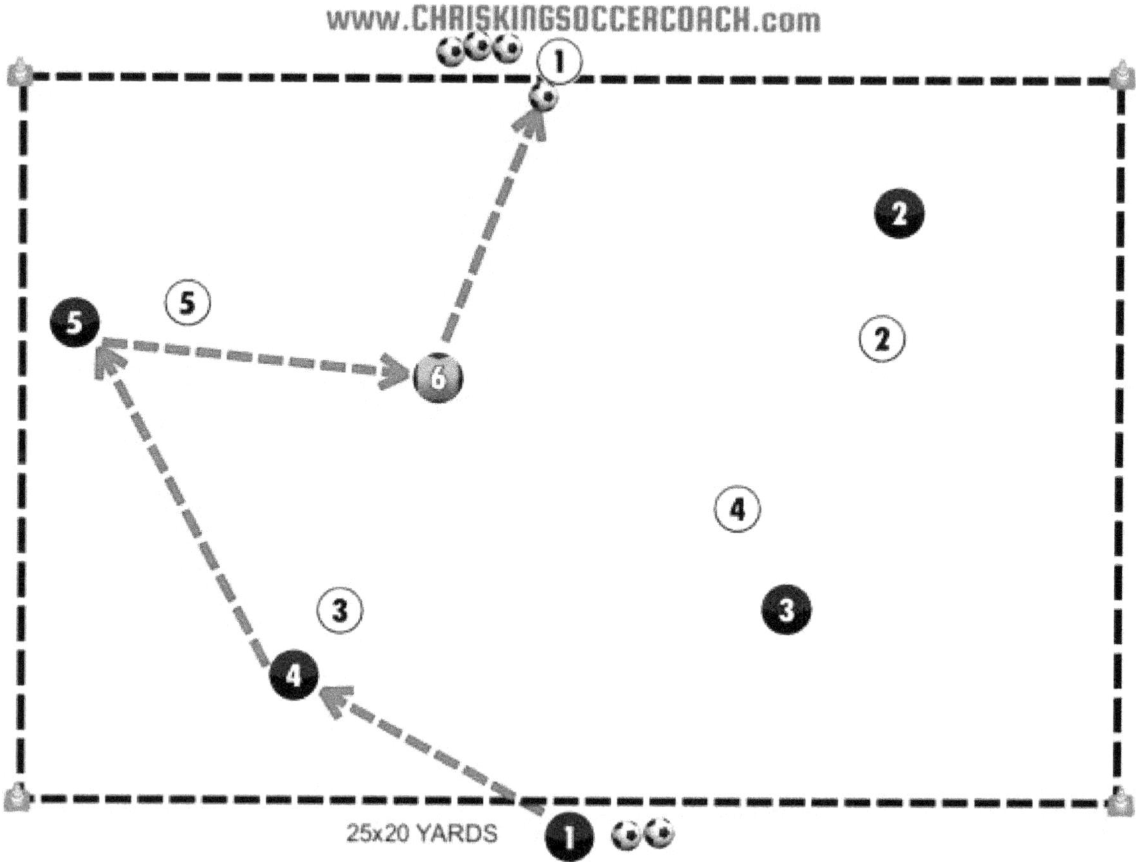

CHAPTER 14
SESSION 4 DRILL 3:
PLAYING FROM THE BACK LINE TO THE FORWARD LINE

PURPOSE:

- Improve the team's ability to move the ball effectively from the back line in a controlled build up, through the midfield to the forwards.

SET UP:

- 16 Players (alternatively between 13 and 20 players: add or remove players from each team as needed. The main focus is to keep the back four shape & practice building up through them)
- 8 Discs
- Size: About 3/4 of a full size pitch
- 20 Minutes

THE DRILL:

- The pitch is split into three thirds - play always starts and restarts with the goalkeepers.
- Black goalkeeper plays out into the first third in which two defensive players (Black #1 & Black #2) and one attacking player (White #7) are only allowed inside. This rule only applies for the team in possession in their defensive third. Once they move the ball into Zone B they can move forward to make it six players in Zone B (as the Whites have done in the first image).
- Attempt to build up through a good back four shape into the final third and score. If a team scores they keep the ball and play restarts from their goalkeeper.
- If the defensive team wins it, they should make fast transitional movements and change from their defensive set up to their attacking formation.

KEY POINTS:

- As per the image, make sure to have a good back four shape when the goalkeeper has the ball. This should be: #1 & #2 are wide apart from each other in the defensive third so they provide options and are hard to mark. #2 & #5 are outside the defensive third (Zone A or C) and are high and wide to provide options and stretch the opposition.

COACHES NOTES:

- When the ball goes out to one full back, the opposite full back tucks back in slightly to avoid large spaces in case the ball is lost.

- If the ball switches from one side to the other, the opposite full back gets wide as the ball switches over.

- If the opposition team wins possession, get into attacking shape quickly.

Starting Shape: As per Drill 2, Black (in possession) is in a good back four shape. The full backs (#3 & #4) are high and wide, the centre backs (#1 & #2) are split so the opposition have to choose who to mark. Black #5 is making himself available to receive the ball.

(Image: Session 4 - drill 3 - A)

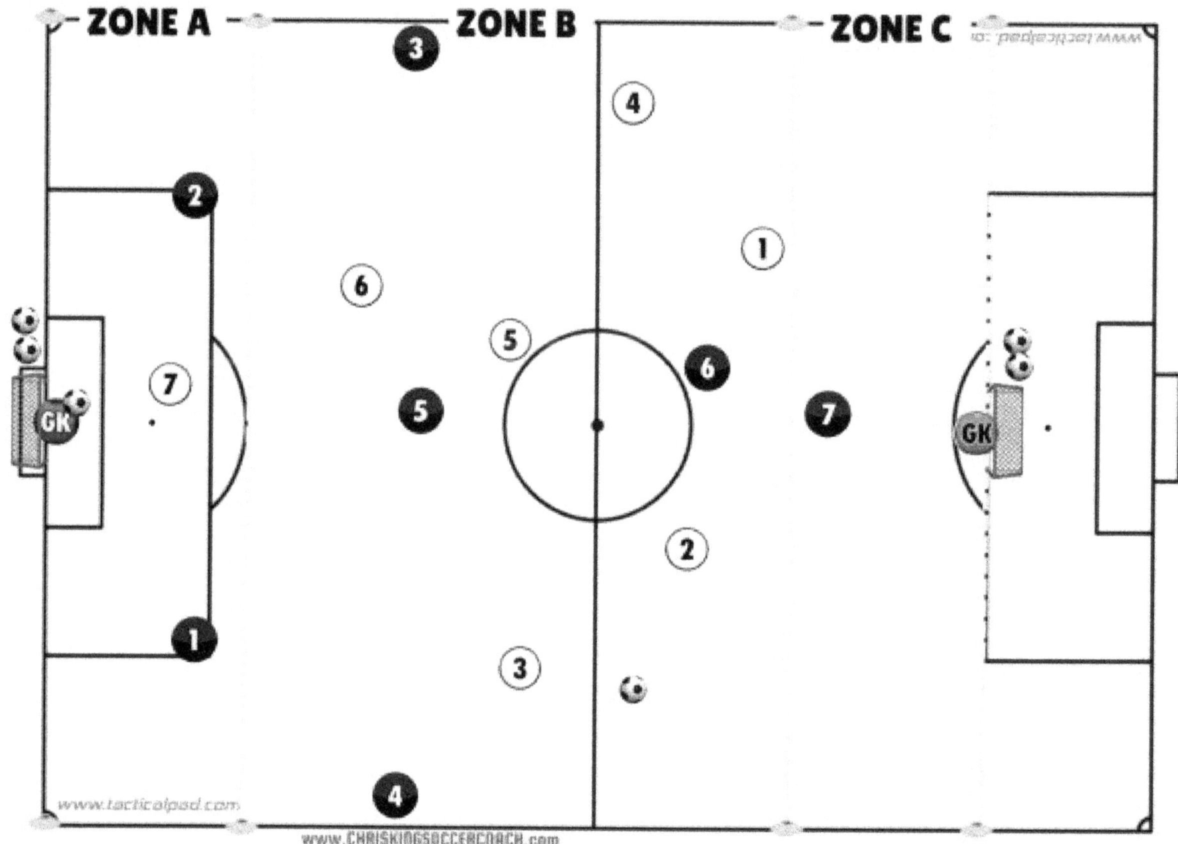

In Play: The goalkeeper has played it to the centre back (Black #2) who has dribbled and passed to his full back (Black #3). Notice how the Black's shape changes as the ball moves. Black #4 pushes up slightly, Black #5 and Black #6 get in positions to support the ball carrier. Black 1# tucks in for now to balance the defensive shape (if Black #3 gets past their player then Black #4 can push higher up). And Black #7 times his run to be an option.

At the same time, the White team has to readjust, mark their players and try to block off passing lanes.

(Image: Session 4 - drill 3 - B)

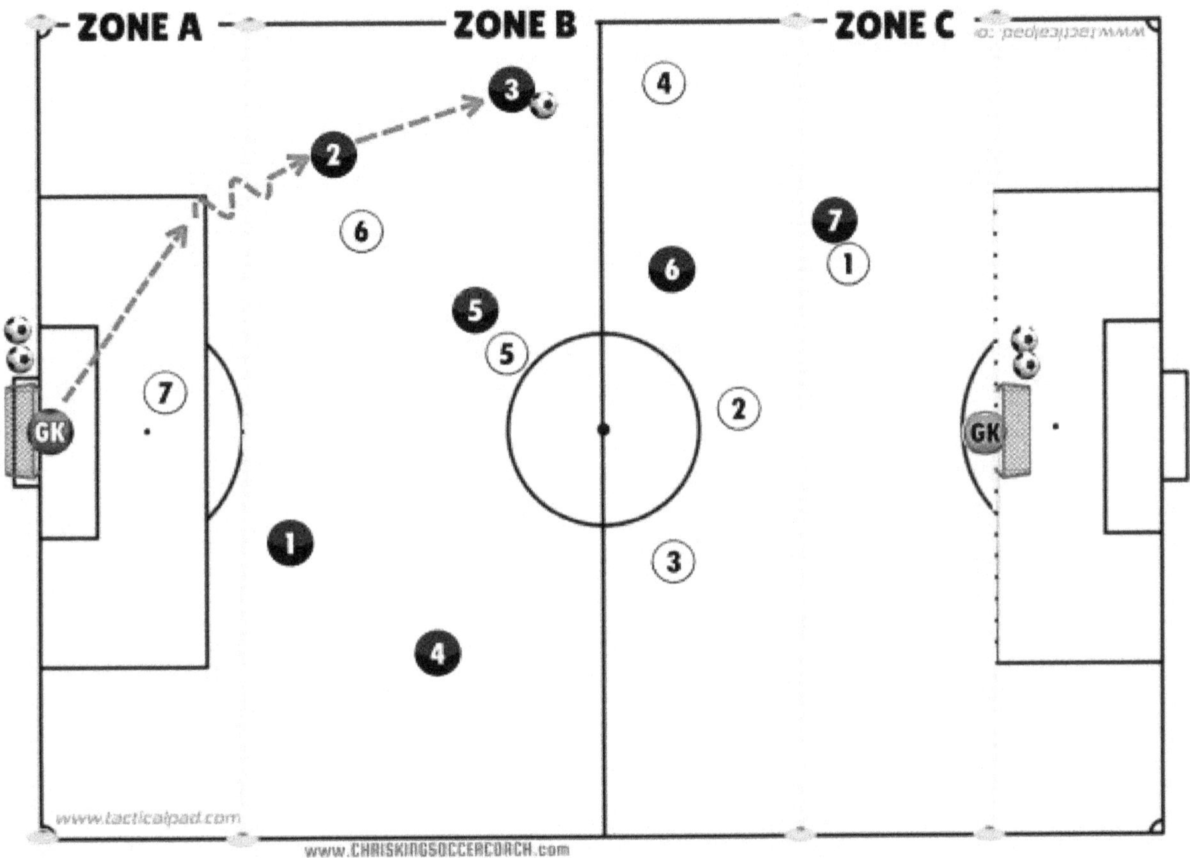

That's all of the drills for this book.

It will take you and your players a couple of run throughs to work on what you are trying to achieve in each drill. But with practice will come speed and quality and your team will greatly improve, as will your coaching.

On the next few pages, there is some general advice on how to run a better session. It's things that I've found help me to be more organised, relaxed and productive when coaching, hopefully you will use a few of them.

CHAPTER 15

TIPS ON HOW TO BE A BETTER COACH

I'll admit I'm not the most organised person in the world. But when it comes to coaching a team or club you have to be prepared! If you're not an organised person by nature, learn how to be on the training track. It will save you a lot of time and you'll enjoy yourself more and you'll run a better training session.

Here's the big one: **Don't wait until 30 minutes before your session starts to plan what you are going to do.**

I know life gets in the way, but simply spend a bit of time the night before or earlier that day/week to choose which session you're going to run.

Use the drills in this book (or other soccer books/videos) and the advice below and you'll be fine, it'll only take you 10-15 minutes to plan a session.

Then, on the day of the training, simply refresh yourself with it for 5 minutes before you arrive at training. (Once you get to training, if you're a head coach you will have other players and coaches asking you questions, so have a quick look at the session while you have time to yourself, even if it's in the car once you arrive at training).

You will find you will be a more relaxed and effective coach if you have spent time planning prior to arriving and this will show in your session.

Okay, with that out of the way here are some other tips for you...

Set your drills up prior to the session starting

If you have access to the ground prior to your training starting time, have as many of your drills set out as possible!

I can't stress this enough. Step out your distances, put your cones down, have your bibs put down in the appropriate areas of your drill, bring out the small goals, have the balls spread around the drill. You get your players for approximately 90 minutes of good quality training, so don't waste 10-15 minutes of it setting up drills during a session while your players get cold and bored.

Have enough balls

If possible, have 10-15 balls (assuming you are training 12 to 14 players).Don't just have 3 balls which the players spend half their time chasing around. Do you think Andre Agassi won Grand Slams because he had one tennis ball and he retrieved it every time he miss hit it? No. His father bought a ball machine and fired hundreds and hundreds of tennis balls at him. Then they collected them when they needed a quick break.

So have as many soccer balls as possible on hand so the players get maximum value out of the drill. When the balls run out, get all the players to stop and collect them and go again. Or alternatively, get two of the juniors to stay behind and be ball boys/girls for the night and give them a free can of pop.

Players training gear in the one spot

If the players need a drink or they need to put on a top, you don't want them going miles away. Get them to put their drinks, spare boots, tops etc that they may need in the session close by in the one area so they are not running off for minutes at a time in all different directions.

Use flat discs on the field

Use a normal cone to mark the outside of an area, but if you need to mark out a square or line inside the main area, use flat discs so the players and balls aren't hitting cones. They cost $5 for 10 from a sports store and will save time and frustration.

Keep all your gear separate from other coaches

Sorry to sound selfish, but if at all possible, keep a ball bag with all your balls and another bag with bibs, cones and discs either at your place or at the club but don't let other teams use it. I know this may not be possible due to lack of funds at a lot of clubs, but if at all possible take most of your gear with you after each session. If this isn't possible, even if you just buy some bibs and cones and keep those separate so you're not running around prior to training wondering where they've all disappeared to. You will be glad come next training session that you have all your gear with you and not here, there and everywhere.

And lastly...

Don't over explain a drill

Don't spend 10 minutes going through every detail of a drill with the players - most of them lose concentration. They will learn by doing.

Simply give a quick 1 to 2 minute explanation of the drill, the rules and what you want them to get out of it and then say "Right we're live!" and start playing.

Once it's been going for a couple of minutes, then you can pause the drill and reconfirm anything the players are struggling to grasp. This has also given you time to make sure that you've got the drill running as you hoped (if you have to adjust the size of the areas or change players positions etc you can do it now).

Sometimes the longer you explain things at the start, the more confused players become and the more questions they ask. So initially, just have a quick explanation and then start the drill.

CHAPTER 16

WARM UP: FIFA 11+ OFFICIAL WARM UP

For the last three seasons we have implemented the FIFA 11+[1] warm up at our club and we have benefited from it. After two weeks of showing the players what to do, they were running most of the warm up by themselves. The coaches literally set up the cones and then when it was time to start the warm up, simply said "Right, get in your pairs and away you go please".

The FIFA 11+[2] warm up has been shown to reduce major injuries by 50% in recreational/sub-elite football. It consists of three parts with a total of 15 exercises performed in order. It should be performed at the start of every training session.

You should use it as the warm up prior to matches as well but only the running exercises (parts 1 and 3), don't do the core and leg strengthening.

I have inserted an image of the Official FIFA 11 Warm Up in the next page but if you are reading this on a device with a small screen you may struggle, so simply go on YouTube and search "The "11+" Warm-up: Part 1" or copy and paste this link[3]. https://www.youtube.com/watch?v=RSJIp7e7fyY

Parts 1 to 6 & 13 to 15 are the running exercises you should do as the warm up at training and match day. Add in parts 7 to 12 at training to help strengthen muscles but don't do this on match days!

The FIFA 11+[4] program is broken down into 3 parts:

1. Slow-speed running exercises coupled with active and partner stretching (8 minutes) - PARTS 1[5] T0 6 ON YouTube when you search ""The "11+" Warm-up: Part 1"

2. Core and leg strength exercises, along with balance, plyometrics, and agility exercises (12 minutes) - PARTS 7[6] T0 12 ON YouTube when you search ""The "11+" Warm-up: Part 1"

3. Moderate/high speed running exercises integrated with cutting and pivoting movements (2 minutes). - PARTS 13[7] T0 15 ON YouTube when you search ""The "11+" Warm-up: Part 1"

Setting it up: There are six pairs of parallel cones, approximately 5-6m apart. Two players start at the same time from the first pair of cones, jog along the inside of the cones and do the various exercises on the way at each set of cones.

After the last cone, they turn and run back along the outside. On the way back, speed can be increased progressively as players warm up.

The FIFA[8] 11+[9] is well worth implementing. Most of it can be done in a fairly small area and the players look and feel more professional and therefore treat the rest of the session in a more professional manner.

---

1. https://www.youtube.com/watch?v=RSJIp7e7fyY
2. **https://www.youtube.com/watch?v=RSJIp7e7fyY**
3. https://www.youtube.com/watch?v=RSJIp7e7fyY
4. https://www.youtube.com/watch?v=RSJIp7e7fyY
5. https://www.youtube.com/watch?v=RSJIp7e7fyY
6. https://www.youtube.com/watch?v=gf-XEapqXPU&list=PLAPyvPaEZQXmX02V78z-je7e92iLfvD-G&index=7
7. https://www.youtube.com/watch?v=xTPjzXl_QIc&list=PLAPyvPaEZQXmX02V78z-je7e92iLfvD-G&index=25
8. https://www.youtube.com/watch?v=RSJIp7e7fyY
9. https://www.youtube.com/watch?v=RSJIp7e7fyY

On the following page is a breakdown of the exercises that are performed in the first part. I would still suggest going to https://www.youtube.com/watch?v=RSJIp7e7fyY if you are unfamiliar with it as each exercise is shown in a video and explained.

The warm down after a training session or a game should be slow jogging and then walking with intermittent static stretches for approximately 10 minutes.

1. **Straight Ahead**[10]:[11] Jog straight to the last cone. Run slightly more quickly on the way back. Do the exercise 2x.

2. **Running Hip Out:**[12] Jog to the first cone. Stop and lift your knee forwards. Rotate your knee to the side and put your foot down. Jog to the cone and do the exercise on the other leg. When you have finished the course, jog back. Do the exercise 2x.

3. **Running Hip In:**[13] Jog to the first cone. Stop and lift your knee to the side. Rotate your knee forwards and put your foot down. Jog to the next cone and do the exercise on the other leg. When you have finished the course, jog back. Do the exercise 2x.

4. **Circling Partner:**[14] Jog forwards to the first cone. Shuffle sideways at a 90 degree angle towards our partner, shuffle an entire circle around one another (without changing the direction you are looking in) and back to the first cone. Jog to the next cone and repeat the exercise. When you have finished the course, jog back. Do the exercise 2x.

5. **Jumping with Shoulder Contact:**[15] Jog to the first cone. Shuffle sideways at a 90 degree angle towards your partner. In the middle, jump sideways towards each other to make shoulder-to-shoulder contact. Shuffle back to the first cone. Then jog to the next cone and repeat the exercise. When you have finished the course, jog back. Do the exercise 2x.

6. **Quick Forwards and Backwards Sprints:**[16] Run quickly to the second cone then run backwards quickly to the first cone, keeping your hips and knees slightly bent. Repeat, running two cones forwards and one cone backwards. When you have finished the course, jog back. Do the exercise 2x.

You should try not to have long gaps between activities. When your warm up is complete, have a quick break for a drink, explain the next drill and then start.

THANK YOU!

Thank you for buying my book, I hope you got some valuable information from it. I also have a Facebook page and website that I post new drills and information on regularly.

www.chriskingsoccercoach.com[17]

facebook.com/chriskingsoccercoach[18]

Till next time, thanks again and all the best with your coaching!

Chris King

And if you need other coaching books have a look below. I have full coaching sessions for senior players down to coaching kids soccer for parents or volunteers. Just search for:

"Chris King Soccer Coach".

Or sign up for a free soccer eBook at www.chriskingsoccercoach.com[19]

---

10. **https://www.youtube.com/watch?v=RSJIp7e7fyY**
11. https://www.youtube.com/watch?v=RSJIp7e7fyY
12. **https://www.youtube.com/watch?v=rPugh9vf9Hg&t=2s**
13. **https://www.youtube.com/watch?v=dyeV-K5wmQA&t=1s**
14. **https://www.youtube.com/watch?v=67FEXBx_G6g&t=2s**
15. **https://www.youtube.com/watch?v=DlWuFO1e4Xc**
16. **https://www.youtube.com/watch?v=-qLxW9S1CoM**
17. http://www.chriskingsoccercoach.com
18. https://www.facebook.com/chriskingsoccercoach/

19. http://www.chriskingsoccercoach.com

VIEW OTHER SOCCER COACHING BOOKS BY CHRIS KING

Training Sessions For Soccer Coaches Volume 1

Training Sessions For Soccer Coaches Volume 2

Training Sessions For Soccer Coaches Volume 3

Attacking & Shooting Drills For Soccer Coaches

Soccer Rondos Volume 1

Soccer Rondos Volume 2

Coaching Kids Soccer - Volume 1

Coaching Kids Soccer - Volume 2

The Ultimate Soccer Coaching Bundle Volume 1

110 Drills For Soccer Coaches

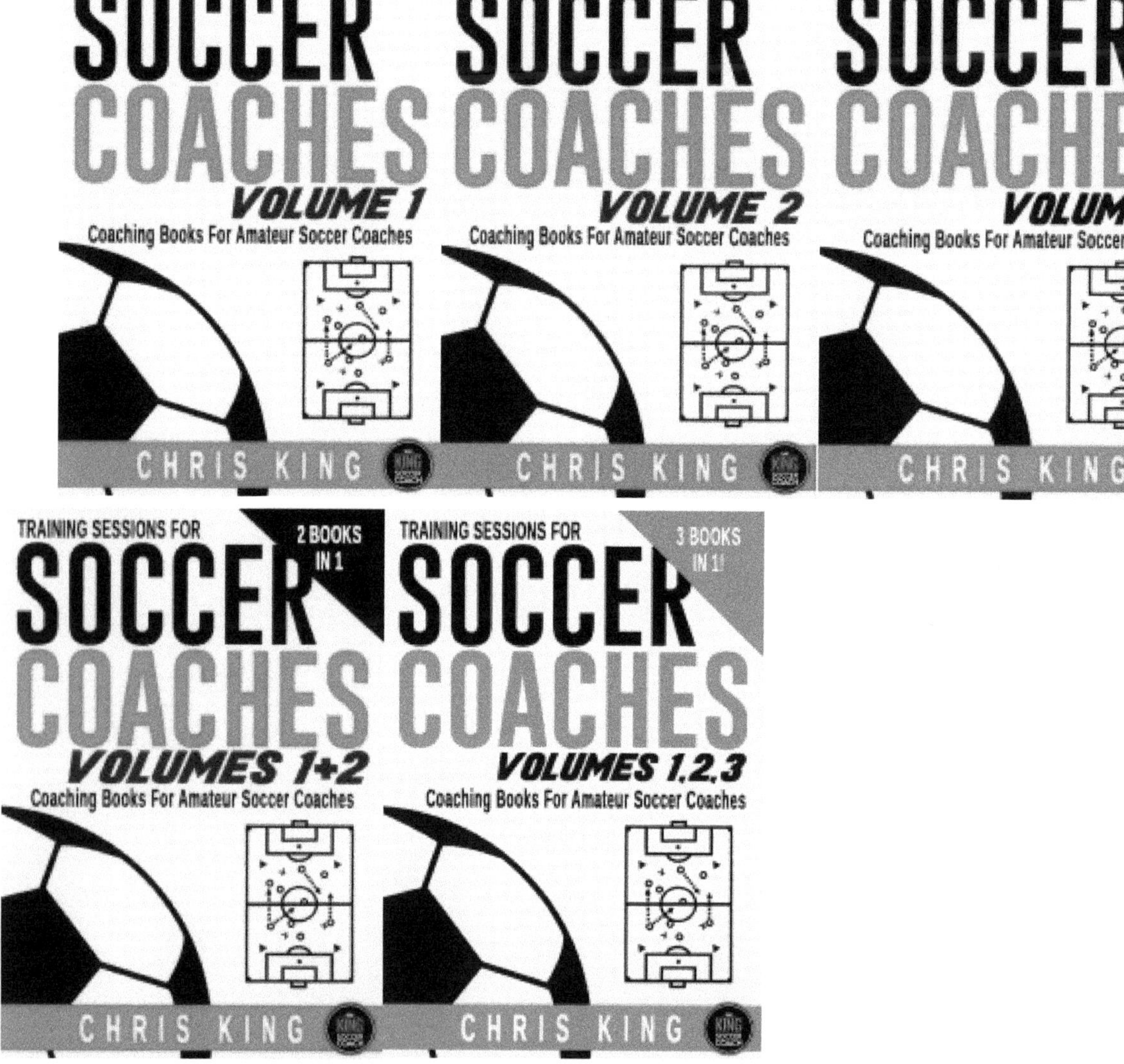

SOCCER RONDOS VOLUME 1
Coaching Books For Amateur Soccer Coaches

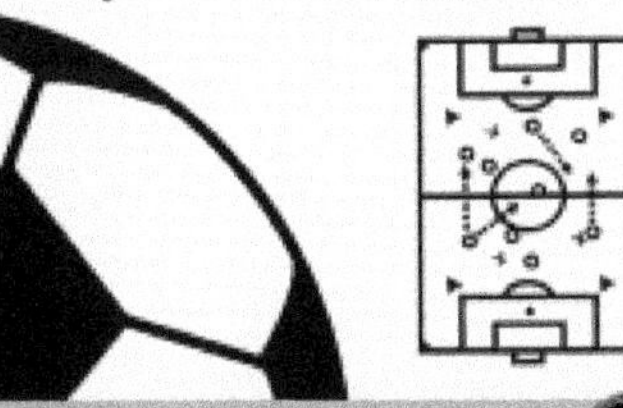

CHRIS KING

SOCCER RONDOS VOLUME 2
Coaching Books For Amateur Soccer Coaches

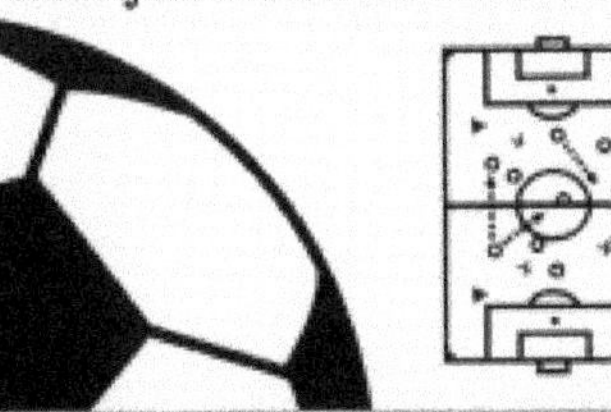

CHRIS KING

VOLUMES 1+2
Coaching Books For Amateur Soccer Coaches

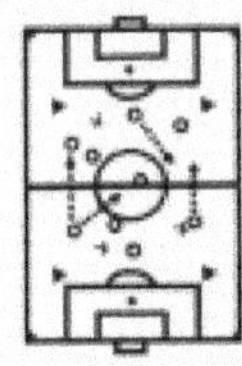

CHRIS KING

COACHING KIDS SOCCER
AGES 5 TO 10
VOLUME 1
This book is for first time coaches, volunteers, parents and anyone wanting to coach!

Set up simple, fun and effective drills and organise a training session in 5 minutes!
CHRIS KING

COACHING KIDS SOCCER
AGES 5 TO 10
VOLUME 2
This book is for first time coaches, grassroots coaches, volunteers and parents!

Set up simple soccer drills that teach kids skills while having fun!
CHRIS KING

VOLUMES 1+2
This book is for first time coaches, volunteers & any would be coach

Set up simple, fun and effective drills & organise a practice session in 5 minutes!
CHRIS KING

ATTACKING & SHOOTING DRILLS FOR

CHRIS KING

THE ULTIMATE SOCCER COACHING BUNDLE
5 BOOKS IN 1!
VOLUME ONE
CHRIS KING

110 DRILLS FOR SOCCER COACHES
7 BOOKS IN 1!
Coaching Books For Amateur Soccer Coaches

THIS BOOK INCLUDES 7 BOOKS IN 1!
CHRIS KING